Play Poker to Win

Play Poker to Win

BY "AMARILLO SLIM" PRESTON
with Bill G. Cox

GROSSET & DUNLAP
A National General Company
Publishers   New York

This book is dedicated to my darling wife, Helen, and my three children – Bunky, Becky, and Tod

"Amarillo Slim" Preston

To my wife, Ruth, who helped so much

Bill G. Cox

Contents

Preface

I PLAY POKER to win.

I've been doing that in places all over the world for years. It's the way I make my living — I'm a professional gambler — and I've won and lost sackfuls of money at the poker table; but I've won a hell of a lot more than I've lost.

I won the World Series of Poker in Las Vegas, Nevada in May, 1972, and, neighbor, at one point I had a better chance of getting a French date with the Statue of Liberty than I did of winning that tournament. In fact, with $80,000 on the table divided between the remaining players in that elimination game, I was down at one time to $1,700, while a spectator behind the rail was betting 25 to 1 that I wouldn't win. Of course, I took that bet. It gave me incentive, but I really didn't need any more with all of those black $100 checks already on the table. A little later, I graduated to being an 8 to 5 underdog, and I took some of that, too.

I've played poker in every sizable city in the U.S., and in just about every casino and elite private club in Europe, the Orient, and South America. I go anywhere for a big game because I thrive on action. Don't get me wrong—I like the money, too—but it's the challenge and thrill of matching wits with and beating the best poker players in the world that turns me on.

A wire-service reporter once described me as a "walking encyclopedia of what's going on in gaming circles," I guess that's true, but another newspaperman caught my exact feelings when he wrote in a story about me: "He plays constantly, devotedly, joyously, wholeheartedly, and with passion — as certain consecrated artists practice their art." He might have added that poker is my nourishment: My six-foot four, 171-pound frame that long ago earned me the nickname of "Slim" doesn't require much actual grub to keep it going.

I make no bones about being a pro — and the men I gamble with are pros — the cream-of-the-crop, blue-ribbon players — tops in their fields whether it's low-ball, hold'em, stud, or razz.

Yet the same principles of play followed by the high rollers also apply if you're playing in the average American weekend poker session, in the home, or at the country club.

Sure, the power of the cold bluff is restricted in a game with a limit. But just as important for the players in a home game as for the pros in a World Series showdown are things such as psychology, position, figuring the price of a pot, spotting a "tell," trapping (and all trappers don't wear fur caps), selling and betting a hand, and knowing the hidden percentages of poker.

I don't mention hunches because I don't believe in hunches; hunches are for dogs making love.

I was a pool hustler before I was a poker player. It was a hell of a good education for what was yet to come, not to mention that it made me some money. I became the champion snooker player in my hometown, and later

I travelled around the globe, beating some of the best in the business. But pool wasn't lucrative for very long after World War II. Poker was.

Poker was an offshoot of my pool-shooting days. Not all gamblers who hang around pool halls bet on the pool games, you know. That's how I started playing cards in my late teens, because I'm a dude who likes to bet on anything competitive. (In past years, I've bet big money that I could broad jump further than anybody on a golf course, that I could pick any thirty people at random and two of them would have the same birthday, that a stray cat that wandered into a swank club was so smart he could carry an empty coke bottle across the room and set it on the cash register, and that a champion checker player could never trap my one king with his two kings, no matter how many moves he made. I won every one of these bets.)

All of the town's poker studs regularly beat the hell out of me during the early days. Those guys would break me every week, but I was learning, neighbor. And practical experience is the best experience. Back then, I'd lose my ass on a pat 10 in a lowball game. If a fellow did that to me twice, I'd snap to it. I learned to adjust to my mistakes.

There have been some good books written on poker, but most of them have been by college professors, or by people who have run something through computers. The advice that I have to offer on how to play smart, winning poker comes from thousands of hours spent at the poker tables, with big, big money at stake.

I had to learn to use my eyes and my ears, and, neighbor, I can see a gnat's keester at a hundred yards and hear a mouse wet on cotton. I'm also pretty good with head arithmetic, which some people call percentages and odds. But most important of all, I have learned to like and to know people. I can go back anywhere I've ever played.

Today, there are more card players in America than there are golfers, bowlers, and tennis players combined. Not all of these card players play poker (bridge, canasta, gin rummy or Old Maid may be their thing), but a large number of them likes to sit behind the chips, whether it's for pennies or fortunes.

The following pages contain the lessons I've learned in some of the world's biggest poker games. It's information you can put to use next Saturday night and come out a winner.

I had a friend once who gave me a lot of advice. Being young, I sometimes wondered if he knew just what the hell he was talking about. A mutual friend assured me that my adviser was a man of his word, as a good gambler must be; and a gambler's word is his stock in trade. "If he tells you that a goose will pull a plow," said this cohort, "Then hook him up, because he'll damn sure move it out."

1

The World Series of Poker

WHEN THE EIGHT of us started playing at the poker table, I damn sure didn't think that halfway through the game I'd be a 25 to 1 underdog, with only a handful of chips keeping me in the competition.

I doubt that there's three to five percent difference in the playing ability of the men filling the chairs in this contest, the final tournament of the 1972 World Series of Poker. We're playing hold'em, a variation of seven-card stud, and the stakes are $80,000 — one winner take all, plus the world champion poker crown.

The players, going left around the table, are Texas Dolly, Jimmy Casella, Crandall, Pug Pearson, Jack Strauss, Jolly Roger, yours truly and Johnny Moss (Johnny was the winner of the World Series of Poker the year before).

We draw cards for seating position. During the hours ahead, we don't touch the cards other than our own hands. A senate dealer — a sharp guy we consider the best in the business and who knows damn well he can't make any mistakes — deals the cards.

We're spread around an oval, green-topped table with a slightly raised black edge to keep the checks from falling off. The upholstered chairs are comfortable, but no one is napping. The action is taking place in a roped-off corner of Benny Binion's plush Horseshoe Hotel casino in downtown Las Vegas — Glitter Gulch is what downtown is called — as compared to The Strip out in the county. The daylight-type, indirect lighting of the casino never changes, and you never know if it's day or night. There are not any clocks.

Above us — the silent, watchful eye of a TV camera focuses on the table, relaying the play to closed-circuit TV screens all over the casino. Another TV camera zooms in for a face closeup of one of us. But we're not thinking about those cameras.

The kibitzers behind the velvet rope — we call it the rail — are quiet. The faces will change, but the crowd will be there throughout the grinding hours of this showdown game. It reminds you of the hushed galleries of a golf tournament. A floor man gives a sporadic spiel about the progress of our play.

Only the press and the casino executives are allowed in front of the rail. The press boys better be legitimate press, too, because we don't want anybody close to the table who shouldn't be there, for obvious reasons.

In hold'em, each player gets two down cards. Three cards are turned face up in the center. Later, two more are dealt face up, one at a time, with the betting coming after each turn of the cards. The five cards in the middle are community cards, to be used by all of us. From this total of seven cards, the best five are played for a hand.

Under our rules, we start with a $10 ante, with a force-in being optional. (A force-in means you bet in the dark, or without looking at your hand. The advantage of the force-in is that when play gets back to you, you still have raising privileges.)

The World Series of Poker was originated by Benny

and Jack Binion, owners of the Horseshoe in Vegas. In 1968, they called a meeting of about fifty of the best poker players in the world at Reno, Nevada to talk over the idea of a World Series. The first year we had it, there was no overall winner. (About 150 invitations to play in the 1972 World Series were mailed to card players all over the world.) Some of the newspaper guys came to me and wanted to know how we could call it a contest if there wasn't a winner. That was a good point. So I suggested a freeze-out type arrangement, where each player posts a specified amount of money and can't quit until he's either lost it or won the whole wad.

We started playing competitively in 1970 — not that we hadn't always been as competitive as hell as far as the money was concerned; and there were several divisions: lowball, stud, hold'em, and seven-card high. A winner emerged from each division and an overall champion was named. (Moss was the first.)

In the hold'em division, the change-in per man is $10,000, no more, no less. The ante starts at $10, but the minute that two players are busted, it goes up to $25, then to $50 in four-handed, and up to $100 when two are left. The force-in is optional, but it can't be less than $100 because of the high ante.

Although eight players start now, twelve people originally had posted their money for hold'em. Four had to drop out and withdraw their bundle because they stayed too long without sleep in an earlier game. The stakes in some of these preliminary games we play compared to the World Series games are like minnows next to whales.

Four hours after we begin, gray-haired Jimmy Casella, who yaks about as much as I do while he plays, squints through the smoke-haze of his ever-present

4

cigarette. The flop has turned a six of clubs, a six of diamonds, and a queen of diamonds in the center. *Jimmy's got the king, ten of diamonds in his hand. Naturally, he's going at a flush, and he's got an overcard, the king.* *

Casella leads off and bets. Pug Pearson, so named because of his nose and who I think is the best all-around poker player anywhere today, doesn't raise *although he's got queens full on sixes. He had two queens in the pocket.* Not wanting to stool his hand, he just calls. *He's got the winning hand* — nothing can beat him with the exception of four sixes, and if he's up against four sixes, he's going to go broke anyway holding that full house.

The next card off proves to be a misfortune for Jimmy. It's a four of diamonds. *It makes his flush, and seals his doom.* He leads off and bets. Pug calls with no raise, hoping to break this other guy behind him, Jack Strauss, who's as dangerous as a rattlesnake on a rock. But Jack tosses in his hand.

The next card off is a blank. Casella passes, *thinking now that his flush might not be any good.* But Pug moves in on him, and Casella calls with all his checks. That busts him out. This doesn't take anything away from Jimmy's playing, because you might as well be the first man out as the last man out; you come away with the same amount of nothing.

The game moves along, and Crandall gets his business in trouble. Crandall, a Texas millionaire who dresses immaculately and changes his entire outfit three times a day, is a soft-spoken, likeable guy. I'm out of this hand, but I watch it closely. The flop has come a five, six, eight. I'm guessing Crandall's drawing to a straight or

*Unknown cards held by players are italicized for clarity.

a pair. *He's got a seven, eight in his hand, and the turn gives him two eights or an open-ended straight; or he can catch another eight and win with trips.* Strauss has a hand, and he and Crandall put in all their checks. *Strauss has two tens in the hole. Now millionaire Crandall's got a million-dollar hand working: There are four fours he can win with, four nines, two eights, and three sevens. He can catch a seven and make two pair — sevens and eights.* The next two cards are blanks and, in the showdown, Strauss's tens beat Crandall's eights. So two players are out.

With six players remaining, we cash in the $5 checks, drawing high card until someone winds up with $25 worth of the $5 checks. Meanwhile, my good friend Johnny Moss has run his checks up pretty good. *Johnny has two deuces in the pocket.* Texas Dolly, a mammoth-sized gent of 294 pounds who won a state track record as an outstanding college athlete, leads off. *He has two aces.* Four people call.

The flop turns a two, seven, nine.

Texas Dolly is first action and he bets. Strauss calls it. *He's got a nine and a jack, which gives him two nines with a jack kicker.* Now it gets to Mr. Moss, who raises it *with his three deuces.* Texas Dolly studies his hand a long time. He probably figures he's going into a concealed hand because it wasn't raised going in. Somebody could have nines and sevens or three nines or three sevens, or he could have what Johnny has (*three deuces*).

After more deliberation, Texas Dolly says, "Well, if these things aren't any good, I'm ready to get out." So he calls. Strauss folds, knowing his hand is not any good at this point.

Texas Dolly and Moss look through the discards only. Sure enough, there's an ace gone in the eleven cards that are out — counting a burned card and the ten cards of the other five players. So Texas Dolly is dead in the pot unless he gets the remaining ace. The dealer burns one, turns one, and it's a ten; he burns one, turns one and — it's that case ace!

Texas Dolly puts a terrible drawout on Johnny Moss.

After that, we rock along, and a hand comes up between Pug, Jolly Roger and Johnny.

Pug has got two kings in the pocket. He raises it. *Jolly Roger has two nines.* He calls. *Moss also has two nines. This means the hands of Moss and Jolly Roger are dead unless it comes a five, six, seven, eight out there, which would make them straights.* Moss, after losing that big pot to Texas Dolly's drawout, wants action for his last money. So he moves in. Of course, Pug calls it, and when it gets back to Jolly Roger, he calls it. I don't blame him for doing that because now the pot's laying over three to one. They run the cards out and Pug's two kings win, knocking out both Moss and Jolly Roger. It's pretty unusual to bust two players in one hand.

Pug, Strauss, Texas Dolly and I are the survivors. The cards fall for a new round. I've got the queen, and ten of spades. The flop turns a ten of clubs, four of spades, and seven of spades.

Now I've got a monstrous hand: Two tens and four spades to draw at, and I'm glad I'm wearing that big-brimmed Stetson of mine. (No one's ever spotted a "tell" on me that I know of, but a man's eyes show 90 percent of what he's thinking; when I'm wearing my hat, you can only see my eyes when I want you to. Some players wear dark glasses.) With what I'm holding, I wouldn't be much of an underdog if one of these cats has two aces; with two cards to come I can catch a spade for a flush, or a ten and make trips, or a queen for two

7

pair. Ordinarily, with a ten, queen of spades in the pocket, I'd shoot this pot up, but I've got bad position for a raise.

My bearded friend, Jack Strauss, a six-foot-seven exbasketball player who seems always to fidget in his chair, limps around in there and catches something. I figure him for two pair. *It was sevens and fours.* But I still think my hand's about equal to his.

Why? Because there are two tens, three queens, and nine spades in there that will make me a hand. So I have fourteen winners out. With two cards to come, that's twenty-eight cards that figure to help my hand.

The turn comes. The nine of diamonds hits. The last community card is an ace, which doesn't help either of us.

So Jack doubles through me. His two pair win nearly all my checks. I lose $11,200 in this pot, and that gets me to counting my chips; I usually know what's in front of me, but now I count them anyway. I've got only $1,775 left, with the rest of that $80,000 divided among the other three, and I couldn't be much worse off. It takes chips to win at poker.

One of the reporters whom I'd taken a genuine liking to saunters over. He looks damn glum, and leans over saying "Slim, a man at the rail is laying 25 to 1 that you don't win it."

"Well, I'm taking $100 of that," I tell him with a grin. I really don't feel like grinning because I realize I've got the worst of that bet. It's a helluva lot higher price than that, as far as the odds on me winning the tournament. I've got to be a 40 to 1 shot with the small pile of checks I've got left. But still, $2,500 to $100 intrigues me, so I latch on to that side wager.

The action moves along without much change.

Comes a pot and I'm the first in, so I darken it for $100 (a force-in). Texas Dolly calls the $100 and plays for $700. Pug and Strauss both call the $700.

So far, I've got $100 in there and only about $1,700 worth of checks in front of me. I barely glance at one of my cards, noticing that it's a king. I shove back my hat and tell the boys, "Well, there ain't no need of me looking at that other card. I can get action for my money *now*. It makes no difference what that other card is." I push in all my checks.

I'm guessing Texas Dolly's got a fairly high pair. *He has a pair of tens.* Pug and Strauss call my $1,700. The flop turns a five, five, three. Texas Dolly, who's got the lead action, bets $4,000, and Jack and Pug drop out. I'm already all in. Well, I look at my other card and damned if it's not a five of hearts. The trips beat out Texas Dolly's pair of tens.

The $5,200 I win here picks me up; it could be the turning point for me. But I'm still a big underdog; I've got less than $7,000 in chips, and the others have got $73,000 among them.

So we rock on.

It comes a raised pot to me. It's raised $700 by Pug, who doesn't raise very many pots. He's been trying to sit back and trap with a hand so the rest of us will raise with almost anything, and he'll break somebody with a concealed hand.

Jack calls this raise from Pug. I glance at my hand and see the ace, king offsuit. Now that's a big hand in hold'em.

So I lay the lash to it — I shoot this thing way, way up. Texas Dolly's got a snowball; he folds. Pug stalls and stalls. I'm thinking, "I'm gonna run into a hand with this boy."

9

I always try to determine what my opponent has early in the hand, before the turn. After that, it's a bluffing proposition with me.

Pug finally calls. "Well, lookee here," I think. "Pug's got himself a scored pair — say, sixes, sevens, or eights, huh?" I know if it's two queens or better, he'll play back at me.

Jack also calls. Then comes the turn. It comes a king, three, four. Pug passes. Jack passes.

Since I'm holding ace, king, I've got two kings with an ace kicker. I do some quick calculating: If I catch somebody with a king, queen in his hand, I've got him dead to a queen. If I catch somebody with two tens, well he's dead to a ten hitting.

So I've got what's considered a million-dollar hand in hold'em. But that's the fascinating part of this game — its versatility; there are so many concealed hands that can be made. If one of these boys has two treys in the pocket, he'll make trips on me. But I've got a reputation for picking up people's money, so I make a pretty good-sized bet.

Pug calls it.

Jack, who's played with me more than Pug has, thinks I have exactly what I do. He folds. Later when the hand is over, he tells me exactly what I held, without ever having seen the cards. That's why that boy is so dangerous.

Now I figure Pug for a good hand. *He has a pair of tens.* Pug doesn't think I have a king, so he calls me. Off comes another trey; making me kings and treys, with an ace kicker. That ace is a very important card in my hand for this reason: You must play five cards. If I run into a man with a king, queen, I'm going to win this pot. He'll have kings and treys just like me, but he'll have 'em with a queen kicker.

The next card comes off — a nine spot. I still feel awful good.

Pug checks it.

I bet him $5,000.

He calls.

He loses with tens and treys.

After that hand, it's beginning to be a long night's day. It rocks and rocks along. Now it seems like it's Texas Dolly who's winning all the big pots.

Meanwhile, all of us sitting here except Jack Strauss are hoping that Jack will be knocked out of the game. Understand, it's nothing personal; it's just that Jack is the damn most dangerous hold'em player — besides me — that there is. He's liable to break you with a deuce and a seven.

Finally a pot comes up between Texas Dolly and Strauss. Strauss has the best hand, but Texas Dolly's got a good draw. There's talk of laying and taking insurance (a player can bet on the side to cover his game loss, although insurance money can't get into the game under the World Series rules) on this hand because Jack has all of his money in. *Jack has a nine and a seven; Texas Dolly's got a nine and a ten.* The fall in the center is six, seven, nine. *Texas Dolly's drawing at a straight, and although he's got the worst hand, he can win if an eight hits.* And it does. So far, Texas Dolly has done the best drawing in the game, because Jack is the second player that Texas Dolly's busted out drawing to his hand.

By now, we've been up a long time. This is the last night of the World Series and an awards banquet is on. Going in for the awards is the only formal break in the

11

long game: Under the rules, a player can be away from the table for thirty minutes to go to the head or grab a bite to eat; after that he must put $100 into every pot until he gets back. So there are no two-hour lunch breaks.

It isn't long before Pug, Texas Dolly and I are back at it. The game's getting fast. Besides anteing $50 each, all three of us are forcing the pot for $200, which amounts to a $350 ante before the cards are dealt.

I'm at my best during fast play. If one of these cats weakens to me, why, goddamn him, I'll take his money. If you show any weakness at this table, there'll be a seat open where *you* were sitting mighty quick. Show any weakness in your voice, in your actions, and you're gone. Here, I'm not only going to make them guess if I got a hand (and guessers are losers, neighbor); I'll make it look like a bluff if I do have a hand.

I look down in a minute and see that I've run that scrawny $1,775 up to $22,600. I'm now just a little shy of having a third of the checks on the table. Texas Dolly's got the most, Pug's second and I've still got the least.

At this point, a friend of mine drops by. He looks a little anxious. He says solemnly, "Say, Slim, a man just laid me $8,000 to $5,000 that you don't win it."

"Well," I say to myself, "the odds are getting a little better anyway."

"This guy says you got it back up in pretty good shape," my pal explains. "He thinks you're probably the best player left in there, but you're still on the short end of the chips."

"Well, my God, boy — I'm really pulling for you to win it," I tell him with some flourish.

"You better be, damn it — you got half of it!" And he walks off.

So here's my predicament: This friend has bet an extra

$2,500 for me on my winning, and I didn't even have a chance to say if I wanted that side bet. My motive is really growing, with that $2,500 to $100 bet I took earlier, plus what's on the table.

The play goes on. By now I've whittled down Texas Dolly to $20,100. And suddenly, Texas Dolly is sick — I mean *real* sick. He's running at both ends. We all agree to a thirty-minute break. It soon becomes obvious to the casino executives that Texas Dolly can't continue in the game because of illness. Under the World Series rules, he would forfeit his money, and he readily agrees to this. But he and I are past partners, and I don't feel like taking $20,000 off a guy with whom I've done that much business: Pug and I talk it over and agree to continue with the chips that are on the table, letting Texas Dolly keep his $20,100.

With the playoff down to the two of us, the ante goes up to $100. Pug, by the way, is an ex-pool hustler like me, but we've got different poker styles. I clown a lot when I'm playing, and I'm always yakking with the kibitzers at the rail; which irks the hell out of Pug, since he knows it is part of my psychological strategy in poker games. If I can get a guy to listen to me, it will be to his misfortune.

"You better play 'em tight, you skinny son-of-a-bitch, because I'm going to break you before the night's over," Pug warns.

I give him a big grin. "Take your best shot, partner. I been broke in bigger towns than Vegas, and lost to better men than you."

But Pug's making the best hands now. I don't make nothing. And if I try to steal a hand, he calls me.

"I like you, Pug," I tell him, "but I'll put a rattlesnake in your pocket and ask you for a match."

This brings a scowl and a grunt.

It's not going well for me. I guess I'm a little fatigued; having played for two days and two nights in another game before this one; with only about six hours sleep between. So I take my first break at the snack bar and order a glass of buttermilk. Then I go to the little boys room and piss off about half of those seventy cups of coffee I've drunk during the game. I douse my hands and face in cold water, which perks me up a little.

I get after Pug. We've been anteing the $100 and darkening it for $200. If Pug puts in $200, I put in $400. The way we are playing, it's always up to him. He huddles with some of his cohorts and I hear one of them tell him "that Slim son-of-a-bitch is straddling you every time you come in — you can't let him do that and win." Now, this is true. You can't stay straddled and win.

After this advice from his pals, it's soon evident that Pug means to take charge. After I put in $200, he comes out with $400 all of a sudden. So I top that with $800 in the dark — and that's unheard of.

I've got $1,100 in that pot and don't even have a hand.

Pug can see that to straddle me it will cost him $1,600, and he doesn't care to play that fast. But I'm a fast player: I'd play a banjo when a game's short-handed. So I'm making my fast game work for me. If I have a hand, I raise; if I have a cold bluff, I raise. The way Pug plays tells me a lot. When he has to give first indication on his hand, I figure it this way: If I've raised it — and it comes a king, queen, and a trey on the turn — and Pug decides to play, I know within reason that the king or queen hit him, since I raised the pot going in. If he passes, it doesn't make any difference if I have an eight and a four — that king is not important to me — I bet him $1,500. During the head-knocking between us, I'm all in — all my checks — on seven different hands. Pug never has all his chips in.

The kibitzers are not quiet now. The floor man narrating the game; although he's no Howard Cosell, has them whipped up. He's droning, "Amarillo Slim's a-movin' in."

In a minute, I push it all out again and this guy hollers, "Amarillo Slim's all in again!"

I yell, "It feels better in!" and the crowd roars with laughter.

One time I feel sure that Pug is going to break me. I make an awful big bluff at him: He bets me $5,200 and I raise him $12,000, with no hand. I can't beat an egg, and I know he's going to call. I believe it's the first time that he senses I don't have a hand. It's the first time during all of this that he ever counts out his chips — the exact amount of checks to call the bet.

"My God Almighty," I'm thinking to myself. "I hope he don't call." But he dogs it and throws his hand away.

Another one of those cliff-hangers comes up, but he pitches in the best hand. Of course, that's the mark of a good player: anybody who can't quit the best hand can't play. But now I feel that he's going to call me the next big bet that I make.

Everytime I move in, the floor man shouts, "Amarillo Slim's a-movin' in, and it feels better in!" Chill Wills, the western actor who's been sitting beside me through quite a bit of this, hollers to the crowd, "Who are we rootin' for?" and they yell back, "Amarillo Slim!" I guess this isn't exactly fair to Pug, but hell, people always cheer for whomever they want at a sporting event.

I'm playing fast and taking Pug's money when I'm holding no hand at all. Jimmy "The Greek" Snyder, who used to write a syndicated column and who's now a public relations man in Las Vegas, leans over and whispers to Pug. I've got mighty keen hearing. The Greek tells Pug I'm taking the money without a hand.

I make up my mind at this point: The first time that I make a hand — what I think probably is the winning hand — I'm going to sell it to him real high, playing it just like the bluffs I've been taking him with all along. When the turn comes, I get the king of hearts, jack of clubs. *Pugs holds two sixes.* The pot's raised and re-raised, with $1,400 above the ante in there. The flop turns an eight, eight, king. I'm first action after the flop. If this boy's got a hand now, I'm going to break him. So instead of making him a sensible bet, like $1,500 or $2,000 — I move in, betting him $51,000, although ordinarily, you wouldn't sell the hand that I had anywhere nearly that high. You might sell it for $2,000 and then quit if you get played back at; but knowing he was fixing to call me the first time he got anything because he knows I've been running bluffs, I decide to use this to my advantage. Pug doesn't stall long: With $8,900 left, he covers that much of my bet, and he's all in for the first — and last — time.

The dealer turns the last two up cards. The first one off is an eight. Now Pug's dead in the pot. The last card is a blank that means nothing. Now I've made eights full on kings, which ends the game for Pug and his eights full on sixes. The entire game has lasted thirty-eight hours.

There's confusion everywhere now — cameras going off, microphones stuck in my face, people slapping me on the back, laughing, shouting.

Later, they tell that I showed the first real jubilance I'd shown in the game: I always act happy as hell when I'm playing anyway. I get to a phone and call my family in Amarillo; I yell "I won it!"

It's about three in the morning. I'm standing outside the Horseshoe; the air is hot and dry, and there aren't many people outside, except those still milling around the Horseshoe. I'm already a little disgusted: I've been looking two hours for another game.

My reporter buddy joins me. I push my hat back and sigh. "I'm looking for a game — any game at all, as long as it's for real money. Seems like a feller should be able to get a game like that — something interesting, you know — in a town like this. But I swear to goodness I just can't find a thing to occupy my time!"

"Goddamn it, Slim, you just won $60,000 in the World Series of Poker!"

"But that was *then*, and this is *now*. Feller like me, he's kind of like a doctor or a lawyer: You know, pretty near the only stock in trade that he's got is his time."

Psychology of Smart Poker

PSYCHOLOGY IS A fancy word, but you don't have to be a licensed psychologist to practice it in poker.

I'll give you an example of applied psychology. Ironically, it happened when I wasn't playing poker. As I've said before, I've been known to speculate on anything that's competitive.

One day, I was playing golf with some gambling buddies in Amarillo, Texas, where I grew up and still live today. Among the golfers was Big Jim, who always was thinking up something different to bet on, especially with me. Big Jim turns to me and, taking the toothpick he is chewing out of his mouth, says "Slim, you think you can outrun anybody that's here on the golf course right now?"

"You're goddamn right I think I can, buddy." You can see I have never been shy, and I did have a reputation for being a fairly fleet-of-foot cat. In fact, I had outrun some good athletes on past occasions when money was riding on the outcome. I once even ran a footrace with a quarterhorse, which is about equal to racing the wind; and I won it, too.

Although we continue to play golf for a while longer, I can hear the wheels turning in Big Jim's head. I also notice that Big Jim's caddy is a long-legged, loose-jointed kid who floats on his feet and impresses me as being able to outrun a gazelle.

I begin to limp a little. "Damn it, Jim," I say. "I hurt my heel somehow on that last hole. I don't think I can run a race. But I tell you what: I'll bet you that I can broad jump further than anyone on the links right now — you name him!"

"You really think so, huh?" Big Jim hitches up his pants and gets kind of a dirty, cat-that-ate-the-bird grin on his face. He glances at his stilt-legged-kid caddy, and adds, "Okay, you're on." Then he steps away a few feet and draws a line on the grass. "This will be the jumping line." he says.

"Hold on a minute, partner," I interrupt. "Since this is a golf course, let's jump from behind a golf club." As I say this, I lay down an iron.

"Why the hell you want to use a golf club?" Big Jim asks. He's trying to figure if I've got a gimmick, and if I do, what kind.

"I just think it's more in keeping with the surroundings. What's it they say — when in Rome, do as the Romans. I've also got a stipulation that's got to be made before this is a bet: If either jumper even *touches* this golf club, he's disqualified and loses the money. All right?"

Big Jim doesn't see anything wrong with that, so he nods in agreement. Now, it doesn't take a Nobel-prize scientist to figure out that Big Jim's entry will be this caddy of his. While I limber up a little, getting ready for the big jump, Big Jim and his buddies are huddling close by, pooling their money to make additional wagers. I sidle up to this caddy, who looks to me as though he could jump further than a goosed frog. I bend over to tighten my shoe laces, saying to him in a low voice:

21

"Let me give you some friendly advice, kid. Big Jim and those friends of his are tough babies, and if you accidentally lose them a bundle of money, why, my god, they're just as liable to kick your ass all the way down to the creek and back. Of course, if you lose because I outjump you, that's a hoss of a different color — but just don't accidentally touch that golf club!" I move off without waiting for him to say anything as Big Jim comes up to talk to the kid. The kid's eyes are getting as big as basketballs. A few of Big Jim's words waft over on the breeze ". . . and if you do, you little bastard, I'll stomp the hell out of you!"

We flip a coin to see who jumps first, and I'm the one.

I get a good start and give it all I got when I spring, making pretty good distance, which is then marked.

Now I watch the kid. It looks as if he's dropped back a whole city block. Then he's running like hell — he's just a blur, and I'm very glad I'm not racing him. Suddenly the guy leaves the ground, a good two yards behind that golf club! Even then it looks to me like he's going into orbit. When he comes down, even after that two yard safety margin he took, he's barely a few inches behind my jump. I collect the money, but, neighbor, I'd never have won it without a little applied psychology.

I learned how to use psychology in poker. Using it, you have an edge that can make the difference between winning and losing. In fact, I play the *players* more than I play the *cards*.

If you're going to win the money, psychology is as important as position at the table, the odds and percentages involved in making a hand, knowing how to price the pot, or running a trap.

Psychology of Smart Poker

Good poker psychology is based on two things: intelligent observation, and common sense. Psychology also calls for old-fashioned ham-acting and some high-pressure salesmanship. If you put it all together right, you'll win at poker, whether it is the weekend family game or high-stake poker.

However, it goes almost without saying that you *must* know the people you are playing poker with; if you don't know them, you'd better start studying them, because if you really know and understand your fellow card players, you can decide how to play your hand even before the second turn of the cards. Knowing how the other players play is a fundamental sharp poker strategy.

Here appearances count for everything, neighbor. What they say is true: a man's eyes mirror his soul. So do other physical giveaways, known among professional gamblers as "tells": One player may talk a lot if he's got a hand, giving signs of being anxious to get in; while another player may become very quiet if he's holding something. In my case you can't tell when I'm holding a hand because I talk all the time anyway: I clown when I'm playing (except in merry old England, where they have rules against it). Because of the tells that most amateurs or part-time poker players have, I wouldn't give you a plugged nickel to stand behind these players and call out their hands. They are already telling me through their actions what they're holding.

Now, it's tougher to detect these giveaways when you're playing with pros, but even they are not immune to tells. I have a friend who invariably makes a certain movement when he's holding a good hand, and, as a result, I know when he's there and when he isn't.

Avoid being stereotyped yourself. Don't be a "nine-to-five" type of player; instead vary your style, mix your play up. If you play the same way all the time, then your tells become obvious to sharp players.

For example, if I'm playing stud with a man who's been waiting to catch an ace, king, queen or jack in the hole, I'll beat that cat. You don't have to play with someone like that very long before you see the kind of hand he's showing down and the kind of cards that he is playing back at you with. I am more prone to catch about a six in the hole and try to make a couple of sixes. With good players around the table, you're liable to sell them those two sixes for a lot. And the idea is to sell your hand real high if you make it; you've had to pay something to make it, so sell it as high as you can, because the next one you draw, you are liable to miss.

If you're a tight player, you will tell me that by your bets and your way of playing what you're holding. So the next time you are playing stud and get an ace in the hole and another ace hits you, play it easy. Stall a little before you call a bet: Act like you're wondering if you can win it with an ace high; if you've been playing tight for some time, this can work to your advantage by setting up a trap. The reason is that I will know you as a tight player, and you come in and make a pair of sixes. When a six hits, I don't pay any attention; based on your past method of playing, I don't think the six will help you any. Therefore, you can trap me: you may bust me with that hand. I'm liable to call you with my ace high because I'll put you down as having a king, queen, or jack in the hole: I won't be looking for those two sixes that beat me. Your trap has snapped closed. So beware of falling into a play pattern.

The psychology of a loser is a funny thing. A recent survey showed that about one-half of the people in the

United States engage in one form or another of gambling, whether it's cards, horse racing, football betting or bingo games. This same survey pointed out that the majority of these gamblers are losers. I believe that losing is for the tourists and the suckers. But it seems that most folks would *rather* lose than win; it is as though they are trying to make some kind of sacrifice, to atone for something. In fact, the hidden psychological factor in gambling is that people will stand to lose, but they won't stand to win. I know that sounds strange, but the truth is that if they win, they have to go to dinner. But if they lose, they lose all their money; they cash checks until they bounce, they wire their friends for more money, and they keep on losing as though they are dedicated to it. But if they win, they'll stand to win just a minimum of money.

Not long ago, I had an experience with a loser. I'm at a race track, and a man walks up and says, "Slim, I want to tell my friends that I gambled with you. I'll match you for $100."

I like a little of the edge on any wager I make. So I tell him, "You can lay me $102 to $100, and I'll match you. Otherwise, friend, we'll just have to think of some game of skill".

"What could you think of here?", he asks.

"I tell you what: We'll pitch coins, the closest coin to that wall over there wins."

He agrees, we toss, and I win.

He has a big smile on his face when he hands me the C-note. "Say, Slim, is it all right if I tell my friends I beat you?"

"Why, hell yes, neighbor — it means nothing to me," I assure him as I pocket the $100 and walk off. There's nothing like a happy loser, I always say.

But the difference between a winner and a loser — and don't you ever forget it! — is a matter of what you think of yourself. I believe that you gamble pretty much the same way that you live your life, that you display in games of chance, although maybe in an exaggerated fashion, the same character traits that make you an individual. In the same way that a writer knows his characters' traits, a smart poker player should know his opponents' moves. A writer friend tells me that if he knows what makes a character tick, he'll know his story plot. And I say if you know your fellow poker player, you'll know his game.

Turn the situation around. It never hurts for potential opponents to think you're more than a little stupid and can hardly count all the money in your hip pocket, much less hold onto it. That's one reason that I wear a big cowboy hat, cowboy boots and western duds — especially when I'm globe-trotting and looking for high action. People everywhere assume that anyone from Texas in a ten-gallon hat is not only a billionaire, but an easy mark, a real hoosier. That's just fine with me, because that's the impression I'm trying to leave. This approach puts those dudes in the category of guessers, and guessers are losers in poker, guessers are losers! That's my meat, to make the other guy guess. If a player makes me a bet, it's me who's guessing whether he's got a hand or not. But if this cat makes me a mediocre bet and I play back at him, he is the one guessing. He's saying to himself, "Well, reckon that slim son-of-a-bitch has got a hand or not?" As a guesser, he's at a psychological disadvantage and getting into a situation where I can move in on him fast.

It's important to keep on top of your opponent in the betting so that he'll be first action in the play, the way I straddled Pug Pearson in the World Series hold'em game. When you straddle a guy, you're forcing him to tell you something about his hand.

Of course, no one player continually is going to make the best hand. That's why the ability to bluff, or to sell a hand when you have one, is a major part of strategy. The use of a strong bluff is, of course, less effective in a limit-game because a wise player who's being bluffed knows that he has a maximum number of bets he can lose and call without being badly hurt. Yet everyone knows *some* player who'll stay in every pot, draw to anything and play anything, and this type of cat may not risk keeping a bluffer honest, even if his loss weren't very large.

There are many people who think it's clever as hell to check a good hand, then come on strong later. I think that's a pure sucker play. Even so, just about everybody you know who plays poker who isn't a professional thinks that is the cute way to do it: to make a cinch, check it and then raise. But I can tell you why it isn't. First, if you check a good hand, another man bets, and then you play back at him, chances are that that man's gone — he had a hand that he'd got broke on anyway.

For example, take a lowball game: You make a wheel — ace, deuce, trey, four, five — the lowest hand. You get coy and check it. There's a man playing behind you who made a seven-four. He's going to bet you heavily on that. If you call it, and then move in on him with a raise, he may throw his hand away. But suppose you had led off and bet him·to start with, instead of checking that wheel, then he would have played back at you because he held a good hand. You would have broken that guy.

This very thing happened in a pretournament hold'em

game during the World Series of Poker in Vegas in 1972. I am ribbing Jimmy "The Greek" Snyder to come into a pot. I raise this pot on nothing but nerve; I've got the worst hand you possibly can have: a seven, deuce.

Jimmy says, "I'd sure come in if I had your hand."

"I tell you what, Jimmy. You call it, and then trade hands with me," I tell him.

He does, and I throw him my cards — a real snowball. Then the flop comes a seven, seven, deuce. The Greek has a full house, sevens on deuces. He's got a cinch hand; there's no hand out that will beat it.

Jimmy's first action, and damned if he doesn't pass! *The guy next to him bets because he's drawing at a flush. Another player turns deuces full on sevens, and he calls the guy shooting for the flush. The next card off, this kid makes his flush.*

The Greek checks it again. The flush bets. The guy with the deuces full on sevens raises. It gets back to The Greek, and now he moves in big. As a result, the guy gets rid of his flush and the other man tosses in his full house. The point is this: If The Greek had led off and bet his hand in the beginning, the guy with the flush draw would have raised it, the other full house would have raised it, and all The Greek would have had to do would have been to call the raises. Then, these other cats would have got all their checks in, and The Greek would have broke both of them in one pot. As it was, I think he won about $7,000 on that hand that I'd given to him; but if he'd played it right, he'd won twice that much. (By the way, he gave me a $100 tip after the hand was over, as a courtesy.)

I like to bluff in a high game and leave it to the other players to guess whether or not it is real. I don't like stud poker, but a few years back I was playing in a stud game. This game is six-handed and the stakes are high. I'm the only professional sitting in; the other players are businessmen and part-time gamblers. One of the players — I'll call him The Lawyer (he isn't), is a good friend of mine, but all his life he's had a hard on to beat me out of something. Why he'd rather take me for $500 than win $2,000 from someone else! When he beats me out of $500, he can tell everybody in town and look like a tree full of owls.

The Lawyer drinks some when he plays — not excessively, but he drinks. (I don't drink. I've got nothing against it, but I believe that the stuff is made to sell. And if I did drink, I'd never drink when I'm playing poker.)

In this game, The Lawyer and I are getting in the same pots. Everytime he's in there, I'm in there. Everytime I catch an overcard, I lay the lash to the pot. If The Lawyer's got a nine, seven showing, and I've got a queen, jack up, it doesn't make any difference whether I've got a deuce in the hole — I bet higher than hell.

We're playing along and The Lawyer makes two eights; I have a king, ten up and nothing in the pocket. He leads off and bets those scored eights. I really play back at him, which makes him quit those paired eights.

I make sure that he sees my peewee hole card as I throw my hand away. He knows I took his money with nothing.

We rock along. He pairs tens up. I show a queen, trey. He bets those two tens, and I grab a handful of money and raise him. He can't come up through it; he tosses in the tens. I know that The Lawyer's ass is now getting redder than a trey ball on a pool table. So's his face. He turns purple every time I rake in the pot. Seeing

29

the reaction I'm getting, I think to myself, "The first time that I can get a good hand, I'll cause a spot to be open here."

It's about four A.M., and a big pot comes up between The Lawyer and me. I've got a couple of aces backed up cold turkey. He's got a nine up, *and another one in the hole.* After I fall high with an ace, I lead off with a $50 bet. We're playing fast, anteing $10, which means there's sixty dollars out there at the start. When I bet, another man between us calls and so does The Lawyer; everybody else gets out.

My next card off is a perfect card for me, a deuce. I've got an ace, deuce showing, The other man gets out. The Lawyer has a nine, ten up. I bet and he plays back at me. Here's where I use some more poker psychology: I stall and I stall and I stall. I'm thinking, "Uh huh, this man has got something he's ready to go with." The Lawyer is thinking he has the best hand. I believe that if I'd played back at him right there, he'd have come in the pot anyway. But I only call him.

The next card off to me is a nine spot, which is a good card for me. *With his scored pair of nines, he knows within reason that my nine can't help me much.* He's drawn a seven, giving him seven, nine, ten up. I have the ace, deuce, nine up. But remember, I've got aces back to back; so I pass, knowing that I will get this hand paid off.

The Lawyer doesn't want to lose me; he's trying to milk me like a Rocky Mountain goat. He makes kind of a small bet. "Lookee here," I think, "he's really got what I thought he had." I know by his actions that he's wanting to break me in one pot. So I know now is the time to break this boy; however, if I play back at him, he might gnaw loose, although I don't think he will.

Of course, he might two-pair out on me there at the tail end. It's possible for anyone in the world to draw out, so I don't jeopardize all my checks. Instead, I just call his bet.

During about the last part of this hand, The Lawyer has called over his little, black-and-white pet bulldog Doc, who sit's in his lap while we play. The friendly little bugger seems to be watching the game.

The final card falls perfectly for me — a trey. The Lawyer catches a king. Now I've got these two aces. *He has a pair of nines.* I know that he's either got two nines or two tens, but it doesn't matter, because I've got a mortal cinch. There is no need for me to check this pot to the boy, because I know that he's had about enough of me taking his money without having a hand that he's going to sit still for. Yes, he's ripe for picking.

The thing for me to do now is to make it look like a bluff. So I move in on him. Well, he doesn't hesitate too long. He looks down at this little dog on his lap and says playfully, "Doc, you reckon that bean pole has got any kind of hand?"

The bulldog, goes "arf! arf!"

The Lawyer says, "Me neither, I don't think he's got a goddamned thing!" He sweeps all of his chips out there in the pot.

We show our hands.

The Lawyer picks up that bulldog, leaps to his feet knocking his chair over, and hurls Doc plumb across the room into the wall. I felt sorry for that little dog, but he got up and didn't seem to be hurt as he walked off with his head down.

The whole point of this story is this: When you have a mortal lock on a man, there is no need to tell him. If I play back at him early in such a hand, I lose him or there's a possibility that he'll draw out. That is another advantage of the bluff, too: The fewer people you have in a pot, the less chance you are taking on someone drawing out on you. If The Lawyer had moved in on me early, I would have called him because he is an underdog (no pun intended) with what I thought he held. Yet he could have caught himself another nine or a ten or a running pair and won the pot. But the way I played it eliminated any gamble on my part and broke the man.

So I say this — whether you're a family game poker player or a high roller — when you have a man locked up, there's just no need to tell him. Let him come on in there and when you get ready, you're a cinch to break this person. And, if there is a moral to this story, it's this: Never drink when you play poker, and don't ask your dog's opinion on a hand. As I have said, before, guessers are losers — even dogs.

3
Odds and Percentages – Figuring the Price of a Hand

KNOW YOUR PRICES; that's all it amounts to.

You hear a lot about percentages and odds in the game of poker. Books on this complicated subject have been written by mathematicians, college professors, and expert poker players, based mostly on computerized figures. Intricate tables on problematical poker hands are the results. Well, you can play for ten years, and the same two poker hands won't come up against each other again. Possible poker hands in a fifty-two card deck total 2,598,960 (four suit).

For myself, I like to keep things as simple as possible when pricing a hand. That way, I can concentrate on the players. For example, when you're in a limit game, the price of a hand is easy to figure. The formula: The amount of money in the pot against the amount of money it's going to cost you, compared to the chances of making your hand. There also is a hidden percentage involved, especially in high-stake poker, which I'll explain later.

People are always asking me, "Do you ever draw to an inside straight?". You've heard all of your life that's for the tourists, which ordinarily is true. But there are exceptions to everything.

Suppose that you're playing in a game with a $20 limit.

34

You have started out with a possible hand. With the last card to come you need an eight in the belly to make a straight. Now, needless to say, if there is not an eight showing, you have four eights in the deck and one draw at it. There are twelve other sets of four, which makes forty-eight cards. These forty-eight plus the four eights give you the fifty-two cards in the deck. So the odds are 48 to 4 that you won't catch that needed eight. Let's say that in this $20 limit game there's a $400 pot out there. It can cost you only $20 to get that eight. That's twenty to one the pot's laying you.

If this is a seven-card high game, you can see the majority of the cards already out. Suppose there are three people besides yourself in the pot. Each player has four up cards. That's sixteen cards and none of them is an eight. Subtracting that sixteen from fifty-two leaves thirty-six. Out of those thirty-six cards, then, four of them are units for you. That whittles it down to thirty-two cards (eight sets of fours). The odds now are 8 to 1 that you don't draw the eight. In drawing for that eight, you'll be taking an 8 to 1 risk in a pot that is laying you 20 to 1.

Do I ever draw to an inside straight? I'll damn sure draw to that one.

Whether you can figure the price of a hand exactly depends entirely on the game being played and the number of exposed cards. If I can see the cards, I can tell you pretty quickly the exact price on the chances that you'll make your hand. Now, if it's 10 to 1 that you don't make it — and the pot's only laying you 4 to 1 — then you're a sucker if you come in. You'd be taking 4 to 1 on a 10 to 1 shot. Turn it around — you want to take 10 to 1 on a 4 to 1 shot.

Another good example of this is a lowball hand. Let's

make it wheel lowball — ace, deuce, trey, four, five being the best possible hand. *No. 1 player* stays pat with a nine, seven, ace, trey, four. *No. 2 player* holds an ace, deuce, trey, six, queen. What is the right price for *No. 2 player* to beat what he assumes is a nine, seven pat hand? (No one usually stays pat on a ten.) The only way you can figure these hands, unless you look at all of the discards, is to assume that all of the cards still are in the deck. (Of course, if, because of some clumsy player you have glimpsed a card somewhere, you take one card off, naturally.)

No. 2 player will discard his queen. In order to decide whether or not he can beat that nine-seven, he must figure how many cards that can beat it are out. There are four fours — that is, four cards that will draw out; there are four fives and four sevens, making twelve cards that will draw out. There are four eights and, in this case, four nines. Thus, there are twenty cards in the deck that you can draw that will beat that pat hand.

If these hands were open, the overall figure would be different. You would know that one of your fours, one of your sevens and one of your nines are gone. By the same token, you'd see that two of your possible losing cards have been eliminated: either the ace or the trey in his hand would pair you. But the cards are not exposed, so you must figure on twenty winners for you left in the deck. Since ten cards already are gone (five in each hand), that leaves forty-two cards in the deck. You have thrown away your queen, but since you don't know what is in the other man's hand, you must assume you've got twenty winners and twenty-one losers that are out. So a draw to your six against his nine is 21 to 20 that you don't beat the nine. Remember, you are still assuming he *has* a nine. If the game was seven-card lowball and you could see the hands, you could figure it exactly.

The same system is used in draw poker. If you're holding a deuce, trey, four, five and you're drawing at a straight, you can tell exactly what your price is on drawing that straight. Since you haven't seen the other players' cards, there are four sixes and four aces in the deck that will make your open-ended straight That gives you eight winners, as compared to thirty-four losers, that are out. So it's about 4 to 1 that you don't hit — that's how much the worst of it you've got.

Now, here is where position at the table becomes highly important in figuring your percentages. If you're last to speak and can draw to this hand without a chance of getting raised (this is in high rather than limit poker), then by all means draw, buddy, especially, if there are as many as two players who get in the pot ahead of you, because then you'll be getting damn near your proper price. But the main idea, neighbor, is this: If you make this hand, you'll be getting an additional price. This is the concealed percentage in poker that very few people realize. The concealed percentage is not the 4 to 1 odds that you *don't* make it, but what you're going to win if you *do* make it.

Let's say that two players come in for $200 each, plus the ante — and you shove $200 in there; you're getting laid only 2 to 1 by the pot that you don't make it, which normally wouldn't be good odds at all since you're a 4 to 1 underdog on drawing your straight. But if you do make it and these players have more chips in front of them that you could win, the pot may be laying you as much as 15 to 1 before the betting is over. In other words, let's say you've got $2,000 in checks, and you put in $200 to draw at the straight. If you think you can win the other $1,800 from each of the other players by making your hand, I'd say draw to it. After all, if you don't make it you can't lose that other $1,800.

Count the money that's in the pot. If there are four players in front of you who have come in, then when you get in, the pot's laying you 4 to 1, and the odds aren't over 4 to 1 that you don't hit your straight. But if you're under the gun, that is, the first to play, don't draw at that straight because you don't know whether anyone else will be coming in. You might find yourself against only one player, and that means you're being laid even money by the pot that you won't make your hand. Why in hell take even money on something that's 4 to 1 odds against your winning?

Or take as an example a six-handed stud poker game. You have a four, five, six; the pot hasn't been shot up too high, and you're trying to trap somebody by drawing at this straight. It's a high price that you will not make it.

Try to remember the exposed cards of the players who have tossed in their hands. But you don't have to remember cards such as the jacks, queens, and kings, because they have no bearing at all on your hand. The key cards for you to keep in mind on this four, five and six are the deuces and treys and sevens and eights. See if some of these are gone.

Suppose now that the next card that falls for you is a seven. Now you know that you must catch an eight or a trey. So forget about all of those higher cards. We call this a "cut-across," a term that pretty much means you don't have to fret over cards that don't concern your hand.

Assume that there are three players, including yourself, in this pot up until now. You've seen all the up cards; each of you has four cards. That makes twelve. You can't see the other two players' hole cards, but you can bet a horse that they're not treys. They might be eights, but you can bet a new hat that none of them started in there with a trey in the pocket. You have seen three other cards, too — the exposed cards of the three players who dropped out. That makes fifteen cards known to you (you'd better develop a retentive memory, I might add). So you figure this way: "Well, fifteen cards are out of the deck, leaving thirty-seven cards in. Eight of those thirty-seven are winners for me (four eights, four treys). So it is a little better than 3½ to 1 that I don't make my straight."

Okay, now you can see the price that is in the pot. And this is where you are going to trap somebody. Suppose that one player has a couple of queens. He can see that is a cinch against your hand, and, in all probability, against the other players' hands too. Mr. Two-Queens hauls off and makes you a pretty good wager. The second man falls in also. Now, neighbor, come in because they are going to play you for a pair of some kind and not a very high one at that. So if you do catch a stray eight or trey, you are liable to get your hand paid off. Both of the other guys have exposed pairs or they are paired anyway, or they wouldn't be betting the way they are.

If you catch a trey, the man with the two queens will lead off betting. You're next, and using the bluff, you'll stall a little as though you were wondering whether to call or not. Since he is a good player, he'll be guessing whether or not you made a straight. But you have laid the groundwork for this on fourth street — on that fourth card. He is assuming it is 100 to 1 that you started backed up with a scored pair; otherwise, you don't have much business in that pot. So you make Mr. Two-Queens a big bet — one that is really out-of-line for the pot. If he's a good player, he is going to think, "Uh, huh, he wants me to think he's connected with a straight — he's trying to take my money."

That is what you call playing winning poker. The idea isn't that you're going to make that damn straight, but what's going to happen if you *do* make it. You're liable to cause a vacant chair over there. He may have made two pair, queens up and something. He might have two exposed queens and another one in the hole. He'll really be trying to sell you a bill of goods, and as a result, you'll break him. Remember, it's not the idea that you're bucking more than 3½ to 1 odds that you *won't* make your straight. It is what will happen if you *do* make that draw.

These are your hidden percentages in poker, especially high-stake poker.

There probably are not even forty people in the United States who know the proper percentages involved in drawing out on a hand; but if you do some simple, intelligent figuring, you can do some pretty big winning.

4
High Action Draw Poker
in Venezuela

I'M ON A little business for a casino, on the island of Curaçao, in Netherlands Antilles, which is a rapidly-developing resort area that gets big "turista" play, when word comes to me of a rip-snorting high-action draw poker game, jacks or better, in Caracas, Venezuela. I'm not a draw poker fan, but I'll play anything and go anywhere in the world if the stakes are high enough. To get into this Caracas action, I'll need some proper introduction; and a man I know at the casino here says he knows a prominent horse trainer in Caracas who can help me.

They have very good and exciting horse racing there, another sport that I follow and speculate on. I once owned some race horses myself, but that proved to be a mistake; you should never have a hobby that eats.

It is arranged for me to meet this Caracas horse trainer, so I hop a plane. It isn't very far; I almost could have swum there, since Curaçao in the West Indies is just off the Venezuelan coast. Arriving in the beautiful capital city, I check into a six-hundred-room resort hotel, as fine a hostelry as you'll ever bed down in.

An appointment is set up with Mr. Romero, who they say is one of the leading horse trainers in this country, where horse training is a highly-regarded profession. I can talk easily with people, and Sēnor Romero and I get along right away. He's a smiling, alert-eyed gentleman with the courteous manners usually found among socially-prominent South Americans. He draws on an expensive, long black cigar as we talk, and his dark eyes study me, while I get around to my reason for the visit.

"I'm a professional gambler, Mr. Romero," I say, "and I'm looking for an interesting game. Do you play, sir?"

He chuckles. "It is coincidental that you should ask me, Señor. As a matter of fact, I do play at cards, in an exclusive club here in Caracas. The poker is very high — indeed, you might find it lucrative if you are a man of considerable talents." He flashes his pearly-white teeth.

I give him back his grin. "Well, sir, I'm sure not a cheater, you understand, but I'm a pretty damn good poker player."

He looks just a shade skeptical and studies me in silence. So I put it on. "I imagine everybody in my country thinks of himself as a pretty good player, Señor, and they may be, but I *know* goddamn well I am. And when I do business, I do it above board. So I'll be frank with you, Mr. Romero. I'd like to meet the right people and go sit in this high stake session at your club."

He removes his cigar and gently taps the white ashes into an ash tray, smiling broadly again. "Why, I think that can be arranged, Señor."

Then I say something which I think, for a second or two, may be the wrong thing. "I'll give you twenty-five percent of my play, Mr. Romero."

"Oh, no, no, no, Señor . . . ," he looks up quickly. "I am a good player also. I don't want . . . ."

"I'll give you twenty-five percent of my play for nothing."

His eyes sparkle. Twenty-five percent for nothing seems mighty enticing to this gentleman.

"I think that will be fine," he says, and we shake hands warmly on it.

We're driven to The Club in his limousine, a long, shiny black, ultra-chrome job. A doorman meets us at the ornate entrance, and we walk inside on ankle-deep carpets amid plush furnishings. The Club looks, feels, and smells like money; the sweet smell of prosperity is a smell I enjoy.

I sign my correct name on the guest register — I always sign my legal name wherever I go. That way, after you win, you haven't misrepresented yourself. That keeps down violence, you understand. For example, if you go someplace and you're supposed to be Old So-and-So, an oil-and-gas man from Texas, and then it turns out that you've just got oil on your hair and gas on your stomach — well, there can be poor human relations that follow if you walk away with a bagful.

Mr. Romero, smiling ear to ear and slapping me on the shoulder, introduces me around The Club. I know damn little that's being said because they're speaking Spanish, and just about all I know in Spanish is that "bueno" means good and "pinche" is better.

While I'm meeting all the big-shots and the goody-two-shoes, I'm mentally trying to pick out the poker players. I meet one feller by the name of Gonzales, who, I'm told, owns a chain of resorts around the country. He is a thick-set, impeccably-dressed, suave cat, who wears gold-rimmed glasses. His iron-gray hair is getting rather thin. In broken English, Mr. Gonzales tries to impress me with the fact that he's a big man in these parts, but I already know that from his fancy duds, aristocratic bearing and the fact he's here at this club.

I shake hands with Mr. Alvarez, a local citizen. He doesn't mention what business he's in. He's quiet, spicky-span mannered and I'd guess him to be maybe a clothing store or manufacturing executive. Next I'm introduced to a man named Tony (I just don't recall these people's full names). I notice that Tony, who's younger than the others I've met, is a tennis player because of his tennis outfit.

At the club bar, I have a soft drink and meet a different type of dude. His name's Juan and his looks spell danger: A livid scar runs from the lobe of his left ear clear around his throat. After we shake hands and Juan glares from beneath bushy brows and smiles just enough so that you can hear his face splintering from the effort, I amble off with Mr. Romero, who, in his fine English, explains that Juan is an "ex-bad boy."

"What do you mean, ex-bad boy?" I ask.

"Well, Señor, once they tried to deport him because of his political affiliations, but he controls quite a number of people in this country. He has an unusual nickname — he's known as 'Machete Juan.' But he is a good player in our little games."

Right there, I decide I'll try to beat everybody else before I beat Machete Juan, because he strikes me as the type who takes offense to being loser in a poker game, and I'm not inclined toward violence.

Before my visit at The Club is over, some of the people I've met invite me to be their guest in the jockey club at the horse races the next day, so another little piece of my work plan falls neatly into place.

When Romero drops me at my hotel, I bring up something that's worrying me. "Romero, I need to know for sure what these people are saying. I don't know enough Spanish to order chili."

"I would be glad to assist you myself, Señor, but I will be busy with the horses at the track tomorrow. Perhaps you should employ an interpreter."

"That's a good idea," I tell him as I step out of the limousine. "Why don't you line me up some middle-aged old gal about nineteen or twenty, who can dress up right sharp, be seen with me, and help me know what's going on around me."

In that part of the hemisphere you can acquire just about anything you want for a few American dollars, so my Spanish dictionary was easily found. The next morning my room phone rings; and when I answer, a pretty-sounding, young, female voice informs me that she is my interpreter, and will meet me in the coffee shop. Her name is Juanita, and she's a slim, brown-haired, brown-eyed little lady, a lovely girl who speaks excellent English. I explain her duties, and it isn't long before Romero's limousine arrives to take us to the track.

Juanita fits in immediately as we settle down in the jockey club, for she comes from a nice family. I'm wearing my working clothes — an expensive, tailor-made, Western suit, a pair of $1,000 anteater cowboy boots and a big $100 Stetson hat, along with a bright shirt and loud tie. I make my wagers through Juanita. I don't care about betting too much money on the horses, and yet, if you're looking for the kind of money I want to win at poker, you can't be a $2 shooter at the races. You have to advertise. But when my first wager on the horses is $50, I don't have to advertise it — everybody around there knows it. With a $50 bet down there you get a stack of tickets that looks like a bundle of newspapers on the corner. Right off, I lose it all.

But I'm not worried; I know the right people are watching when I place the bets. Pretty soon Mr. Romero comes up to me. "Señor Slim, I have something good in the fourth race. I am running one of my horses in it, but he is sore. My horse could beat the favorite, but I do not think he will get there." The teeth glisten again.

"What are you trying to suggest, Romero?" I ask.

"Although my horse is a heavy favorite, there is a horse entered that is 9 to 1 odds to win. That horse would be my second choice in the fourth. He will be overlooked a little, at 9 to 1."

I take my friend's advice and put $200 on old Nine-to-One. They're off and Romero's horse, sure enough, doesn't run worth a damn. The second favored horse in the race gets into a little bit of trouble and here comes my horse in.

When they pay off it looks like the national war debt, and I am a big hit in the jockey club. When the waiter brings me a cup of coffee or a soft drink, I tip $2 instead of the usual quarter. I am a sport who wins it and spends it, and that's obvious, I hope.

Between the races, Mr. Gonzales, one of the other club members whom I met the night before, asks me, "Do you play cards as well, Señor?".

"Yes, sir! I'm a real good card player, and I've got the cancelled checks to prove it." He laughs uproariously at this, and then becomes serious. "At our club after dinner this evening, we will get together and play poker. We would welcome you as our guest at dinner and the game."

"That's mighty neighborly of you, Señor. I'll sure as hell be there with bells on."

When the races end, the limousine drops Juanita off at her home and me at the hotel. I don't know how long these cats play in their games, but I like to be

47

fresh in case a session goes on a while. A three-day game is a good tonic for me, and I can play longer if I'm loser.

I hit the sack; and when the ringing phone wakes me up, I don't know how long I've been sleeping. I glance at my watch and see that it's nine-thirty P.M. I've missed dinner at The Club, as planned; but I'll take a little extra sleep over food anytime when I'm getting ready for a game.

The caller is Mr. Gonzales, who wonders if I've had a change of plans. He sounds downright concerned. I make an excuse and apologize and try not to let on this is exactly the way I wanted things — having them want me out there more than me wanting to be there.

I grab a cab, stop to pick up Juanita, and we arrive at The Club thirty minutes later, where I make a new acquaintance, a light-complexioned, dapper little man who's in the coffee business in Brazil. It's obvious that he carries some weight at The Club; he and Mr. Gonzales seem to be the dominating figures, especially in the poker circle. But, in the back of my mind as we head for the poker table, I know that it's Machete Juan I need on my side.

We draw cards for position, take our seats and each player is given a stack of chips. I swivel around to my pretty gal interpreter, saying "Juanita, honey, I need to know how much these chips are worth in money. How much is each color?"

There's some jabbering, after which she tells me in her little-girl voice: "The white ones are $5 chips, the red ones are $50, and the blue ones are $100." I can see that I've got $1,000 worth of checks. With seven players, at the table, that's $7,000.

The players, starting with Gonzales and going clockwise around the table, are Romero, me, Alvarez, Tony the Tennis Player, Machete Juan, and The Coffee Man from Brazil. I don't like to start out bombing people right off when I sit down in a game; I like to leave a good taste with the people I beat, because if you don't the world gets smaller when you leave them and the places you can return to become fewer. That's what a dear friend meant when he told me one time, "You can shear a sheep many a time, Slim, but you can skin him only once." Well I want to shear for a spell. I don't know what kind of players these people are, but I don't really give a damn. My idea is to play the way they play, while we're getting acquainted. I don't know their style of play, or understand their wagering; but I find out that they've got a rule that you can't check a hand and then raise, and that suits me just fine. If I have a hand I'm trying to sell, I'll lead with it, because checking is not worth much, anyway.

We get started. There isn't much talk, and I don't know what they're saying when there is, unless I ask Juanita. But I understand a bet and a raise and a check and a pat and a call, since these are part of a universal language in my trade.

It isn't long before my friend Romero loses all the checks he had in front of him. Now I was waiting for this to happen to somebody, and I wouldn't have cared much even if it had been me. This sounds strange, but I know if I give away this first thousand it's like putting it in the bank. I'll come back the next day and get it, because these dudes don't have to worry about car payments or room rent

Romero loses his butt drawing at a little straight. He makes it, then gets broke. I'm deciding he isn't no player at all, this twenty-five percent silent partner of mine. If I'd had his hand, I might have lost $200 with it, but he loses his whole pile.

This is what I've been waiting to see, though — how much these people will buy after they lose that first thousand. He orders more checks, and I see that most of them are blue: He's bought $2,000 to keep playing. I'm feeling good right now; this is the kind of game I'm after. If a man loses his money, he can get more checks; but, by the same token, I'm wondering about this pay-off thing. I haven't seen any money change hands anywhere. I haven't even put any cash on the line yet.

Soon, Romero excuses himself and leaves the table, and I do the same. In the men's room, I tell Romero, "Tough luck there, friend."

"Yes. Would you have lost that money on that hand, Señor?" It's a pride thing with these people, and this is where my human relations program comes in.

"Hell, yes, Romero. There's no way I could've saved my money on that hand."

"That is what I believed. It looked to me as if it was the best hand."

I agree again, and then broach the subject of the pay-off. By the way, neighbor, how do we straighten these chips out when it's over?"

"Everybody is signing for his chips," he tells me.

"I don't recall signing for mine," I say, scratching my head.

He smiles. "That is all right. I have — how is it you say — okayed you, Señor Slim."

"How do you know you can okay me?"

Smilingly, he explains, "Señor, things are commonly known in Caracas, if one is acquainted with the proper people, that is. Over at the hotel where you are staying, I know what you placed in the safe deposit box." He's congenial as hell about this little bit of information.

I'm some surprised. "Well, who's okaying these other people, Romero?"

"All of them are very honorable men, Señor."

"Then I take it you'll okay anything that I win?"

"Oh, yes, anything that you win, you will get, my friend." He claps me on the back again as we return to the table.

The game rocks along. I whisper to sleepy-eyed Juanita, "Honey, the next time that they mention anything involving an element of time, you interrupt and find out what time they quit playing." She nods and seems to doze off again.

But about fifteen minutes later, she comes alive and shoots off a machine-gun string of words. Machete Juan replies with a glower. "He says that he won't stop until the game is over," Juanita tells me. That's something else my ears have been waiting for, though I'd just as soon hear it from someone besides Machete Juan. But it establishes the three main facts I need to know before I can get down to work: I know that it's a good game — by that, I mean a high game; I know I'll get my money if I win; and I know that if some of these cats are going to be losers, I'll get their eyeballs.

At about one in the morning, the waiters and waitresses bring us a snack, and we back up and eat. I visit with Machete Juan because I figure if anybody's going to try to take the best of the game, it will be him.

The hours tick on. The game gets pretty good. Romero loses some more checks; and The Coffee Man from Brazil (who's delighted with my coffee-drinking habit), loses about $6,000 (I'm delighted with his losing

51

habit); while Tony the Tennis Player has gone broke a couple of times. So there are plenty of chips on the table.

About seven A.M., I can see that none of these cats are used to playing in such a long session. Juanita, bless her pretty little shapely butt, slumbers peacefully in her chair, since I haven't needed any translating for a while. I'd guess these people usually start their game around ten P.M., then break up about two A.M., regardless of who wins or loses. So I know that all this is for my benefit — and, they hope, for their's, too — but it hasn't worked that way. I'm about $7,000 ahead and never have played but one really good pot, where I took $2,000 from The Coffee Man.

A new hand falls around the table. I pick them up — seven, ten, seven, ten, ten. A ten full on sevens.

Gonzales opens, which means he's got jacks or better. *He's holding an ace high straight — ten, jack, queen, king, ace.* Romero calls the $50 bet. *He's got two kings.* I've been watching Gonzales, and I decide he's probably the best player here, besides me, and he's a winner in the game. With these other three players behind me, I see no reason to raise this pot; if Gonzales has a couple of pair or a set of trips and I do play back, he's smart enough to get out fast. So I only call the $50.

Next around is Alvarez, who calls. *He's got fives and sixes paired.*

Next in line is Tony Tennis. *He's got a flush draw — five, deuce, six, nine of clubs and the ace of diamonds.* He calls since he's already got a lot in this game. Machete Juan folds, as does The Coffee Man; *both have busts.* It's back to Gonzales. He stands pat; and I figure he's probably got a pat, too; I've watched him all night and I know what he stays and plays on. He doesn't come in there splashing the water around, and I know he doesn't stay pat on something like two pair and bluff at the pot.

Romero draws three cards to his hand. I'm next, and here I sit with this pat full. I hesitate slightly, although it must be obvious that I'm probably not standing pat on a bust behind a man that's opened and stood pat. But I'm trying to sell my hand to Gonzales, and I know almost for certain that my pat full is the winning hand.

Alvarez, next behind me, draws one card. Tony also takes one. *Romero catches nothing to improve his two kings. Alvarez has some real bad luck — he catches a six that makes him sixes full on fives. And the ace of clubs hits Tony, which gives him an ace high flush.*

The next betting interval, Gonzales leads off and bets $300, which makes me wonder what this boy's holding, since I'm behind him and standing pat. He's figuring me for either a busted hand-cold bluff, or a small straight; because if I'm pat with a full house or flush or set of fours, his hand is no good. Romero throws his hand in.

It's to me now and I'm thinking about raising it. But there are two people behind me, each who drew only one card. They're either drawing to a straight, flush or two pair. So I have no reason to play back at Gonzales at this point, because I'm hoping that one of these guys behind me made his hand. And that he was drawing to a big hand and that he'll bump it. I just call the $300.

Sure enough, Mr. Alvarez *who made his sixes full on fives* plays back at Gonzales; and raises the pot $800. Then it comes to Tony Tennis, who knows that Gonzales stood pat, that Alvarez drew only one, and I stood pat. He probably thinks that if Gonzales and I stood pat with a flush or a straight, his ace high flush is the best hand. Tony calls the $1,100 and shoves in $700 more, all of his checks. When it gets back to Gonzales, he has to come in with his ace high straight. He calls with the rest of his chips.

Now is the time for me to play my full house, but the only player with any money left is Alvarez. *Fortunately, he's got the second best hand out.* I move in. He stalls at my big bet and gets to thinking. I know about what he's thinking: that I can't afford to play back at him like that with a straight or a flush — I've got to have a bigger hand than that. This pot has gotten out of shape, neighbor; and it got that way because of the way I played my hand before the turn. Alvarez calls his last money off, and I break four players in this one pot. It gets real quiet now, because there was real money in that pot. Tony Tennis had the least amount in it, and hell, he'd contributed over $1,700.

We play on for another hour, and the game ends — at their preference, not mine.

Fortunately, Machete Juan, who's a tight player, didn't lose too much money. I still was trying to show a little favoritism to that cat. But after a parting glower, he was gone. The Coffee Man lost a bundle, but it didn't seem to bother him at all.

I won that last big pot that cleaned out four players because I played winning poker. I didn't play back before the draw with that ten full on sevens. If I had, maybe I'd have won one more bet from Gonzales, because he's no fool at cards. He just would have called, surely no more, and the next time around he'd have checked that straight real fast. When you hold a big hand and are up front, don't scare out the people who are drawing. They may draw and do something that isn't good for them, like Alvarez and Tony did.

With the game at an end, there's some excitement

among the small knot of hangers-on, waiters, bartenders, and the like. They crowd around and it wakes Juanita up. I'm sure she's been pulling for me to win, because she knows her salary probably will double if I have a good night. Her wages for the day (or the night) were supposed to be $12. I don't think she had to interpret more than fifteen times during the night; but much to that pretty little gal's surprise, she gets two $100 bills from me, just for helping me out. Her eyes shine like stars in a South American summer sky.

I played one more time with these same players, and the game never did get out of shape. Then, I heard that The Coffee Man would be going to the nearby island of Aruba the next weekend. Just by coincidence, that happened to be exactly where I was going.

I got together with The Coffee Man again in Aruba and played some more cards. It was very, very satisfactory for me.

5
Draw Poker, Jacks or Better

FIVE-CARD DRAW poker is somewhat out of style nowadays. Still, I'm sure it remains a popular game in some circles, especially the family games where Granddaddy taught draw to Daddy and Daddy taught it to Sonny and it comes down through the generations like a family heirloom. Originally, of course, draw was *the* poker game, even with the professionals, but over the years it tended to lose its excitement.

I don't like draw because it's a game in which you must tattle-tale your hand: It doesn't take any wizard to know that when you open, you've got to have jacks or better — that's the name of the game. I played quite a bit of draw when I first started playing poker seriously; and I've won some bundles with it, as I did in that big game in Caracas. So here are some pointers for you old draw standbys.

Position and opening: As in any other poker game, your position at the table (that is, your seat in relation to location of the dealer) determines what you should hold to open. If I were in any of the first three seats to the left of the dealer in a seven-handed draw poker session, I'd never open on a simple pair of jacks. I'd have to have two aces or better if I were up front. The reason I wouldn't come in with the minimum openers is because anybody that I get any business from has got to have those jacks beat. (I'm refering to strong players who know their game.) Stop and think a minute what happens if you kick off a pot with dead-even openers, two jacks. It comes to the next man or so and he calls you. In all probability, he's drawing at something. But if it gets around to the fifth or sixth player and he raises you, he's saying pretty plainly that he can beat your jacks. He wouldn't be raising unless he could beat you, because by the simple act of opening you've revealed that you have jacks or better, and so he's not in the dark.

So, if you open with jacks in the one, two, or three seat, you've got the worst of it unless you help your hand with the draw. After you open, say the fifth man calls and the sixth player really lays some lash to it with a big raise. I don't want any business with him because I know there are only two jacks left in that deck to help my hand, and even if I catch a third jack I might go broke. With only two jacks running wild in there, you have to figure your percentages with the entire deck. If there are seven players, there will be only seventeen cards left for you to draw from. Those two jacks may be in those seventeen cards, or they may be in one of the other players' hands.

So figuring your price you know that two jacks are left in forty-seven cards, since the only cards you're supposed to know about are the five you're holding. You've got two cards out of forty-seven cards that'll help your hand. This makes it about 5½ to 1 that you don't catch the jack. You can see how much the worst of it you've got.

Jacks at the Far End: It's a different story if you're sitting in the fourth, fifth, sixth or seventh chair. In these locations, open with two jacks — if someone could've beat'em they probably would've opened.

It makes a lot more sense to be in one of those last seats and open with a pair of jacks, hoping that you'll catch a running pair or maybe a third jack. And you'll get some business, never fear.

Let's face it, some of the people who play in these weekly games will stay and draw to any combination, whether it's a small straight, a little flush, a pair of fives, or two eights. What's more, they'll draw two cards at these far-fetched possibilities. You're a prohibitive favorite with just your two jacks over anyone that will draw two cards to a straight or flush or small pair. That's strictly for the tourists.

Just about everybody in these amateur games does this — draws to a bust, but if you'll avoid this, you'll be a hardship on these people. And that's the idea when you sit down at the table — you're there to win. Even if the other players are your good friends and neighbors, they're your enemies while you play, as far as "having mercy" goes. After it's all over, you can help them mow the lawn, or give them their money back, if it makes you feel better.

Aces as Openers: Now I'll open with two aces anytime. However, if I get a lot of action, say two people call me and the next guy raises, I'll probably duck those two aces and throw them away, because I don't know what I'm trying to catch. It's a cinch that the guy who raised could beat two aces; I might even get a third ace and still be beaten by the raiser.

But turn it around: If I'm in that back seat holding two aces and someone in front has opened, I'm going to raise. Here's my reason: Besides trying to work out my own hand, I'm trying to determine what the opener has. If he's opened with two jacks, two queens, or paired kings, I've certainly got the best hand. Even if he's opened on two small pair, I'm not the underdog that you might think. Why? Because the opener has to guess whether I can already beat what he's holding. By raising big I might win the pot right there without ever drawing to those two aces. Or I might be called, make three aces, and cause an open seat where the opener's sitting.

Play a Hand Early: I don't believe in legging a hand. You can keep from going broke on a hand if you play it early. Don't wait until after the draw; you can save your money this way.

Say that one player opens with two jacks and I raise, holding two aces, from my position near the back. When it gets around to the field, they all figure on dropping out. If the person that opened has two pair, he'll probably give me the pot, whereas if he's got a straight, he may think that I've got a flush or full house. Since he's guessing, he might not play back at me, but he should with that straight. I don't think anyone plays well enough to save their money with a pat hand *before* the draw; but you can get loose from a pat hand *after* the draw when you see what the other players are doing. But that's why I tell you to play your hand *before* the draw — you just save money.

I'll show you exactly how you can do this. Suppose one player opens with a concealed straight, and I raise him with two aces. When it gets back to him, he moves

61

me in. Well, I'm through with him right there; he's already told me that my two aces aren't any good. (It's now about 60 to 1 that I don't beat that straight, and the pot couldn't possibly be laying 6 to 1 odds. Thus, I've saved my checks with that one raise.)

Take another example with these same hands. The opener stands pat with his straight. I don't raise him, and I draw to my paired aces and catch another ace, a four, and a six. Now I've got to guess whether he's actually got a pat or not, because in draw poker, jacks or better, many a player will stay pat on two pair and bet. Why? Because it's a big gamble that you won't make a full house when you draw anyway. As I've said many times over, the guesser is the loser in poker. In this instance, I'd be guessing whether the opener has a pat or not; and, sure enough, he does. After making those three aces, the average player would go broke with them. I wouldn't, because I'd save my money before the draw by playing back with a big raise and finding out just how strong the opener really is.

Staying on Less Than Openers: Now, if I'm first, second, or third to speak and have a possible straight to draw at, I obviously can't open. Let's suppose, however, that I'm first under the gun and hold a four, five, six, and seven. The next man opens, the following four players call, and then it gets back to me. I'm ready to call it. Unless there's a pat hand out somewhere, I can win if I make my straight.

I know that there isn't a pat hand out, people tell me before the draw what they've got. If one player has a set of threes, for instance, you know he's going to raise and get some checks in there because he can't afford to have all these players drawing and possibly outdrawing his trips. Therefore, since everybody just called, I'll draw at my straight, knowing it'll win if I hit.

When Not to Stay with a Possible: On the other hand, if the player on my left opens, the next two men call, and the following player raises it, then I can't come in with that possible straight, for these three reasons: First, if I call that raise, those other players behind me may have limped their good hands. So if I put my checks in to draw at this straight, the next man calls it, and the third man moves in and raises the re-raiser, my straight probably wouldn't be any good if I made it. (Whenever you put checks in the pot, you've got to think you'll be able to go with your hand.)

Also, I'm out of position; it just reverts to being in poor position, under the gun, first to tattle-tale your hand. However, if that re-raiser raises only a nominal amount, I might call him, because at that time I've got to think my straight will be a winner. Then, too, I'm going to get action from four other players. When that happens, it means the pot is laying me 5 to 1 that I won't make my straight, but the card-draw odds *aren't* 5 to 1 that I won't. I'm talking about a game in which I can bet all my checks, and this is where the hidden percentages come in again. If I make the straight, I can break a player.

Besides, by not being able to open, I don't have a quarter in the pot at this point. There's no reason for me to risk my checks to come in and draw at this "possible." Even if I do come in and make it, I may go broke. So rather than do all this guessing, I know there'll be another deal in about forty seconds and I'll just wait for a new hand.

However, I would play this hand altogether differently in a limit game. I'd go ahead and call this raise and re-raise, knowing there. is a limit on what I could lose. And if I did make it, I'd sure as hell bet all that I could, because I don't draw to any hand that I won't bet. If you draw at something, make it, and check it, then you're defeating yourself.

Never Pass a "Pat" Hand: Say that I'm in the *No. 3* seat. *Player No. 1* opens this pot, then *No. 2* calls, and I look down and see I'm holding a full house. Now most players would get pretty excited with this hand and raise it; but that's not the thing to do, as you saw in the previous chapter, where a similar situation came up in that big game in Caracas.

Don't raise with a full house when there are two people in the pot, coming into you. Just even up call, because those two people in front of you can't beat it, or if they could, you'll lose your money anyway if you get a full house beaten. If you do raise at this time, you'll chase out the other players behind you. In this situation, as it arose in the Caracas game, two players behind me were making one-card draws — one to a small full house and the other to a flush. The guy drawing to the small full house raises for you and he's driving the player with the possible flush and the player with the opening straight right smack into your big full house. That's how the big ones eat up the little ones.

Now, you've probably seen in the movies the fiction

where a guy passes a full house: That's a bunch of crap. You *never* pass a full house. You play it, but just limp in there with it, as though you're not really sure of your hand.

By the way, don't immediately yell "pat! pat!" when you're staying pat. That's a sure tip-off that you *are* holding a pat hand. Act as if there's some question as to how you'll play the hand — that's the real psychology of poker.

Betting in a Limit Game: Let's talk about limit poker and use the same hands that the players held in the Caracas game. These are the hands:

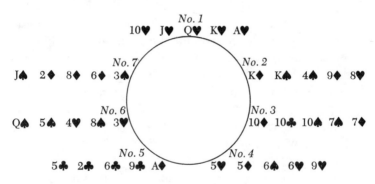

No. 1
10♥ J♥ Q♥ K♥ A♥

No. 7
J♠ 2♦ 8♦ 6♦ 3♠

No. 2
K♦ K♠ 4♠ 9♦ 8♥

No. 6
Q♠ 5♠ 4♥ 8♠ 3♥

No. 3
10♦ 10♣ 10♠ 7♠ 7♦

No. 5
5♣ 2♣ 6♣ 9♣ A♦

No. 4
5♥ 5♦ 6♠ 6♥ 9♥

Player No. 1 — 10, J, Q, K, A — a straight.
Player No. 2 — K, K, 4, 9, 8 — two kings.
Player No. 3(me) — 10, 10, 10, 7, 7 — full house.
Player No. 4 — 5, 5, 6, 6, 9 — two pair.
Player No. 5 — 5, 2, 6, 9 (clubs), A (diamond) — flush draw.
Player No. 6 — Q, 5, 4, 8, 3 — a bust or snowball.
Player No. 7 — J, 2, 8, 6, 3 — a bust.

No. 1 player opens — he's got to with his straight. *No. 2* calls with his two kings. Now, when it comes to me, I do exactly the opposite of what I did in the high-stake game: I immediately *raise* it. Why? Because you must take every opportunity to get some checks in the pot in the game played with a limit, since you can only bet once.

Okay, *No. 4* has fives and sixes, which will cost him two bets (from the opener and me) to come in, but he's aiming for a full house. He calls *No. 5*, who has a flush draw, and he gets in the pot because he already has five bets in ahead of him. *Nos. 6* and *7* fold their bust hands. When it gets back to *No. 1* and his straight, he re-raises it.

No. 2, who isn't a very bright player, calls the raise and re-raise with his two puny kings because he figures, as many a weak player does, that since he's already this far into the pot, he might as well keep going.

When it gets to me (*No. 3*), I raise again. (This depends, of course, on the raise limit, that is, the number of raises allowed.) Players *No. 4* and *5* with their drawing hands call my re-raise, as does *Player No. 1* when it gets back to him.

On the draw, *No. 1* stands pat, *No. 2* takes three cards to his two kings and makes a bust, and I (*No. 3*) stand pat, although stalling and trying to sell my hand. *No. 4* draws one card to his pair, making a six full on fives. Player *No. 5* draws one card, getting an ace and making an ace-high (nut) club flush.

Now *No. 1* bets his straight, thinking it's the winning hand, *No. 2* player, bless him, finally folds. I (*No. 3*) call the bet and raise, and then *Nos. 4* and *5* also call. Finally, *player No. 1* calls, ending the betting. And I win a hatful.

So you see, whenever you have a big hand in limit poker, bet on it as hard as you can. It's safe to lay the lash to your hand, because if you run into people with good hands or good draws, they'll stay; they aren't risking all their chips anyway in a limit game. Whether they are weekend or professional players, once they get into a pot, they usually go on with it unless it gets too fast — and it can't do that in a limit game. You'll make more money raising than you will limping a big hand in limit poker.

I've said that you never should pass a full house, but I'll make one exception to that. Occasionally, after the draw in a limit game when it's down to three-handed, you might "sandwich" a player. That doesn't mean you are playing partners with the third guy; but if you're first, you might check it because you know Old So-and-So over there is one of those tight players, and you know goddamn well that he's got a hand when he comes in, because you know what it takes for him to stay. You can figure that if he's in with a good hand, he's probably going to raise it.

One last bit of advice: When playing high poker against only one player, never draw at a straight. That's for the tourists. You don't stand to make it, and if you do, you're liable to go broke.

Summary Points

- In five-card draw poker your position determines what you can open with. In the first three seats, never open with less than two aces.
- If you're in seats four, five, six, or seven, you can

open with the minimum opener of two jacks, but watch the other hands to see if you should duck these openers after the draw.

- Never, *never* draw to a bust.
- Play your hand *before* the draw and save money.
- Don't draw at a hand that you don't intend to go on with.
- Never pass a "pat" hand, but use some psychology and don't reveal it.
- If you're holding a big hand, bet and raise at every possible opportunity in a limit game. You've got to build up a pot.
- Once players get into a pot, they usually go on unless it gets too fast. However, a strong player knows when to fold a hand.
- Never draw at a straight against one player.

Summary – Five-Card Draw Poker

The following is an analysis of how I won that big pot in Caracas, breaking four players at once:

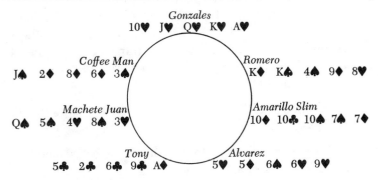

Gonzales
10♥ J♥ Q♥ K♥ A♥

Coffee Man
J♠ 2♦ 8♦ 6♦ 3♠

Romero
K♦ K♣ 4♠ 9♦ 8♥

Machete Juan
Q♠ 5♠ 4♥ 8♠ 3♥

Amarillo Slim
10♦ 10♣ 10♠ 7♠ 7♦

Tony
5♣ 2♣ 6♣ 9♣ A♦

Alvarez
5♥ 5♦ 6♠ 6♥ 9♥

After the Deal:

1st player, Gonzales, is dealt 10, J, Q, K, A — ace-high straight.

2nd player, Romero, is dealt K, K, 4, 9, 8 — two kings.

3rd player, Amarillo Slim, is dealt 10, 10, 10, 7, 7 — full house.

4th player, Alvarez, is dealt 5, 5, 6, 6, 9 — two pair.

5th player, Tony, is dealt 2, 5, 6, 9 (clubs), A (diamond) — flush draw.

6th player, Machete Juan, is dealt Q, 5, 4, 8, 3 — a snowball or bust.

*7th player**, Coffee Man, is dealt J, 2, 8, 6, 3 — a bust.

The Betting:

1st player opens with his ace-high straight.

*Dealer

2nd player stays on his two kings. He is not a good player, but I probably also would have stayed on the two kings, although not for long.

I, the *3rd player,* see no reason to raise this pot with players behind me. I'd scare out Gonzales or perhaps win one bet from him and then scare away the others behind me. I'm hoping to set a trap and get some of these players behind to drive the prey my way, so I just call the bet.

4th player calls the bet, waiting on the draw to his two pair.

5th player will draw to a flush and he calls since he's got a lot in this game.

6th and *7th players* fold busts.

After the Draw:

1st player stands pat on his straight. I figure him for a pat hand, too, because he never comes in splashing water around.

2nd player draws three to two kings, doesn't improve hand, makes a bust.

As *3rd player,* I stand pat, although I pretend to hesitate slightly as though I were unsure. I'm trying to sell this hand to Gonzales.

4th player draws one card to his possible full. Makes 6, 6, 6, 5, 5, sixes full on fives.

5th player takes one to his club flush. the ace of clubs hits, giving him an ace-high flush.

Draw Poker, Jacks or Better

The Betting:

1st player leads off and bets $300 on his pat straight, figuring me for a pat bluff or a small straight.

2nd player folds his bust.

3rd player. I'm thinking about raising it, but there are two players behind me who drew one card each. I'm hoping one of these one-card draws made his hand and that he'll raise. I call the $300 bet.

4th player filled sixes on fives. He plays back at Gonzales, as I had hoped, raising the pot by $800.

5th player knows that Gonzales and I stood pat, and that Alvarez drew only one. He's thinking if Gonzales and I stayed pat with a flush or a straight, his ace-high flush is the winner; so he calls the $1,100 and moves in, betting all the rest of his checks, $700.

1st player has to come in with his ace-high straight. He calls the re-raise with all of his checks.

3rd player. Now is the time for me to move in with my full house. However the only player left with any money is Alvarez (fortunately, he's got the second-best hand out). He stalls, knowing I can't afford to play back at him like that with a straight or flush; I've got to have a bigger hand. But finally he calls with the rest of his checks.

Winning Hand:

Me. I break four players in one pot by legging that full house.

Analysis of Caracas Game Hand
in a Limit Game

After the Deal:

1st player, Gonzales, is dealt 10, J, Q, K, A — ace-high straight.

2nd player, Romero, is dealt K, K, 4, 9, 8 — two kings.

3rd player, Amarillo Slim, is dealt 10, 10, 10, 7, 7 — full house.

4th player, Alvarez, is dealt 5, 5, 6, 6, 9 — two pair.

5th player, Tony, is dealt 2, 5, 6, 9 (clubs), A (diamond) — flush draw.

6th player, Machete Juan, is dealt Q, 5, 4, 8, 3 — a snowball or bust.

7th player*, Coffee Man, is dealt J, 2, 8, 6, 3 — a bust.

The Betting:

1st player opens with his straight. He has to.

2nd player calls with his two kings, hoping to improve on the draw.

3rd player. Seeing I hold a full house, (tens full on sevens) I immediately *raise* it. Remember you must take every available opportunity to get checks into the pot in a limit game.

4th player comes in since he's attempting to fill his two pair.

5th player calls, because he now has five bets in, and he's trying to flush.

*Dealer

6th and *7th players* fold their busts.

1st player raises again.

2nd player calls, (although I don't know why).

3rd player raises once more. (This depends, of course, on the number of raises allowed.)

4th and *5th players* call.

1st player calls.

The Draw:

1st player stands pat with his straight.

2nd player draws three to two kings, makes a bust.

3rd player. I stand pat, although trying to seem a little hesitant.

4th player draws one to his two pair, makes sixes full on fives.

5th player draws one to his club flush, gets an ace, and makes an ace-high club flush.

The Betting:

1st player, thinking he holds the winning hand, bets with his straight, wanting to build the pot.

2nd player finally folds.

3rd player. I call and raise.

4th and *5th players* also call.

1st player calls, ending the betting.

Winner:

Me. I ran the pot as high as I could by raising all I could.

Hold'em

HOLD'EM, A VARIATION of seven-card stud, is my game. I play it better than any other kind of poker, and, needless to say, I'd rather play it than anything else. I don't think you can find a game more filled with excitement, or one that involves a greater element of luck, and yet demanding that you do some damn smart figuring if you want to succeed as a hold'em player.

In hold'em, no hand is a mortal cinch to win until that last card falls. In fact, what started as the best hand may end up being the worst because of the many combinations possible in this intriguing game.

For some years now hold'em has been a top game among the high-stake gamblers of the country; I know, because I've played with all of them — in the East, West, North, and South. It is also known by other names, including Hold Me and Hold Me, Darling. Today, I think hold'em is on the way to becoming the most popular poker game in America, even at that once-a-week family get-together around the table, because it's a game that can be just as much fun with a nickel ante and a quarter limit as when high table stakes are riding on the outcome.

It's a simple game to play, but a complex one to master. In the first place, a different set of values is involved on the hands that can be made, compared to the same hands in other poker games: The turn of one card can make a monstrous hand into an underdog.

I'm going to give away a few trade secrets in this chapter, but a word of advice, neighbor: Read this closely and study the examples carefully. Then get a deck of cards and practice; deal out the hands I'm talking about and really get the feel of them. Study the combinations and the possibilities, and then read over the chapter a few more times.

If you can run a bluff, hold'em is your game, because there is a greater element of bluff in hold'em than in any other poker. Lowball, for instance, is not much of a bluffing game, simply because it's hard to misrepresent a hand that's concealed; whereas in hold'em, five of the seven cards are exposed on the board.

Hold'em is played in this way: Each player gets two cards, face down. Like any other game, you ante at the start and the first betting interval comes after the first two down cards are dealt. The play rotates to the left of the dealer. On this opening round, a player must stay or get out.

Next, three cards are dealt face up in the center. This is called the flop, and these are community cards to be used by all players in making their hands, along with the two they've got in the hole. You make the second wager after the flop. This time, a player can pass, because a pot's already been started.

Then two more cards are dealt face up in the center, one at a time, with a betting interval after each card. In the games in which I play, we always burn (discard) the top card at the start of every turn — you burn one and turn one. This is a precaution, and the main reason for it is that burning or discarding that top card eliminates cheating about ninety percent of the time (marked cards won't work for a cheater when the top card is burned). We're not accusing anybody of being a cheater: Burning the top card is just a traditional thing in professional and in many amateur games.

Most of the games I play in have no limit, but hold'em is an interesting game to play with a limit, because after the turn there are plenty of times that you'll have something good to draw at.

Here's an example. Suppose you've got the ten and jack of diamonds as hole cards. The turn brings up the seven of diamonds, eight of diamonds and ten of spades (the community cards). Now that doesn't look like much of a hand by usual standards; really, all you've got is two tens. And yet, your hand is a favorite over *two* aces!

Why is your hand — the worst one, obviously — the favorite? Well, neighbor, remember you've got two more cards to come. If you catch another ten, you make trips, and there are two tens left in the deck. Other remaining cards that will help your hand are three jacks: You could make jacks and tens, or even three jacks. Four nines are left, which could give you a straight if one falls. There are eight diamonds that could make you a flush (you've got to say eight because you figured the nine of diamonds as a winner in making a straight).

Add up these helping cards — two tens, three jacks, four nines and eight diamonds — and that's seventeen winners you've got in the deck. With two cards to come you double your chances of drawing a hand, so that adds up to thirty-four winners. With that many winning cards still out, you're damn sure a favorite to beat two aces with that ten, jack of diamonds you're holding.

Now, with you having the ten, jack of diamonds, let's give another player the ace of spades and the ace of clubs. Then suppose that the seven of diamonds, eight of diamonds and ten of spades hit out there in the flop. Your potential draw makes yours the better of the two hands. I'll take your hand and play against those two aces anytime. In twenty hands with these same combinations I'll win the majority of them. I believe that so strongly that I'll take the ten, jack and play freeze-out with anyone, and break whoever is playing against me.

I'd even go so far as to say that any tight player with that two-ace hand could turn his cards face up to me and I'd still call a raise with that ten, jack of diamonds I'm holding. I'm not saying that I'd call a raise with all of my chips, because two aces is the best hand at this point, but I'd call one with up to ten percent of the chips I have in front of me. The reason here is that hidden percentage I've talked about: If I help my hand I might be getting laid 10 to 1 odds that I won't win the pot, because this cat with the two aces will go all the way with them. And I'll break him.

But the picture can change drastically with just one card. If the four of clubs, say, was out there instead of that ten of spades, you're no longer holding the best hand. You've eliminated your two tens.

Now you've got twelve winners — nine diamonds and three nines — left in the deck that can make you either a flush or a straight; considering two cards to come, you've got twenty-four winners. Otherwise, those last two cards would have to be a ten, ten; ten, jack; or jack, jack and the odds of them falling that way are out of this world, roughly in the neighborhood of 150 to 1. So with that four of clubs instead of the ten of spades in the middle, your hand isn't worth anything.

The fourth community card in hold'em is an important one. This card could make a straight or a flush on the board, or in some other way help a player's hand. It's very unusual if it doesn't help somebody. Just to give an example, say the flop includes a queen, jack, five. The fourth up card is dealt and it's a nine. You can bet your horse that somebody in the pot has a ten, giving him a four-card straight draw right there. And if he happens to be holding a king, ten, he's already got himself a king-high straight. Somebody sitting there may have turned three jacks and is feeling good, and suddenly he's looking at a possible straight in another player's hand. That's how much that fourth card can change things.

There are some split pots in hold'em, because with everybody playing those five community cards, there'll be some equal hands held. This is important for you to realize when you first start playing the game. Watch that board and if there's a straight there, everybody that stayed in the pot has got a straight. If the flop cards are seven, eight, nine, ten, jack, and you're holding the queen, naturally you've got the biggest straight at the table. (You don't use the seven, of course.) You've got the winning hand. If no one has a queen, it's a split pot, and everybody that participated shares in the win. Occasionally a four-card flush will come up in hold'em. If there are four hearts on the board and you've got the ace of hearts in your hand, you've got a cinch if the board isn't paired, or if there isn't a possible straight flush out. You'll win with your nut (ace-high) flush.

This is why hold'em is such a fascinating game. You may come in with an ace of hearts and a trey of diamonds. The turn comes a deuce and four of hearts and eight of clubs. Lookee there, partner, you've got some kind of hand! A bigger hand yet would result if the flop included a deuce, four, and eight of hearts. With the ace of hearts in your hand, you've got two draws to make a cinch flush. It'd be a cinch flush because it'd be an ace-high flush. By the same token, if a little, ol' raggedy-ass five hits out there, you've got a straight — ace, deuce, trey, four, five.

There are so many unexpected things that can happen to you in a hold'em game. Let me give another example. A man's sitting there with two eights in his hand, and the turn brings out the deuce and four of hearts and eight of diamonds. Right now, he's got a cinch hand; there's no hand out that will beat his three eights. But boom! Off comes a trey. Now, there are about thirty hands that will beat those three eights. An ace, five will win over his hand, making an ace, deuce, trey, four, five straight. Another winning hand over the three eights would be a four, six, if the player gets a five to go with them. That's just the plain truth — a man drawing may make the cinch hand over the cat who thinks he's already holding one.

Another example of this is a player who has paired kings in the hole (his two down cards), and the turn brings out the king of diamonds, seven of clubs, and eight of hearts. He has to play these three kings: They're a strong hand; but at the same time, this is a dangerous turn in hold'em.

With no possible straight or flush showing on the board, any fool can see that three kings are the best hand. Then off jumps that fourth community card, a six. With the fall of that six, somebody holding a nine and ten will beat your hand. If a player holds that nine, ten, it's even money that he stayed in for this turn anyway because that seven, eight already on the board is damn near as good as you can get to a nine, ten draw; it gives you all the sixes and all the jacks to make a cinch hand and with two draws at it.

Now, if the man with the three kings leads off and

bets, the player with the nine, ten can either play back at him or let it go with a call. But if Mr. Nine-Ten lets it go, he's jeopardizing all of his checks. My own action would be to play back at the player with those three kings because if that man figures to go broke, he'll put some lash to that hand. If Mr. Nine-Ten doesn't play back and that last community card is either a six, seven, eight, or king, Mr. Three-Kings makes a full house and Mr. Nine-Ten has waited until his hand was beaten to go broke with it. A big raise from Mr. Nine-Ten might have run Three-Kings out and won the pot, even without another turn.

An important rule to remember: Play your hand fast in hold'em while you're holding the best cards, unless, of course, you've turned some kind of a mortal cinch with which you can afford to psyche some money into the pot. And yet beware of those mortal cinches. By a mortal cinch I mean that if I've got two kings and the turn comes king, seven, eight, I'm going to make a good bet because with three kings, I'm hunting somebody with a draw at something like an ace, king. The ace, king hand will have a shot at two kings with an ace kicker, and I'll sure as hell get a call out of him because he's got the biggest card on the board paired, backed by the ace. Or I might catch someone who took a turn holding a king, eight of spades and is trying for a flush. After the flop he's got kings and eights and you can bust this dude; he's going to play those two top pair there on the board.

So I'll have a strong lead with three kings. If I run into a hand and a man plays back at me, I'll call. I've got the top hand, and he's an underdog if he's shooting at a straight. If he's come in with a king, seven in his hand, he's dead to the pot; if another seven hits, it'll make him a seven full on kings, and, by the same token, I'll have a king full on sevens and cause him some misfortune. In hold'em, you just never know until that final card is turned.

And I'll never forget the time, neighbor, that this was demonstrated to me. I have an expression: "All trappers don't wear fur caps." That came up one time when I beat a feller out of a pot and another player told him, "You let that slim son-of-a-bitch in the cowboy hat take your money." and I told 'em with a grin, "Hell, all trappers don't wear fur caps." But I might have added that sometimes the lambs slaughter the butcher. My thoughts go back to one particular hold'em game when there were seven of us playing, and we got a good pot started. I'm first action and I don't want to tattle-tale my hand because I'm sitting behind the best hand possible on that first turn — two scored aces (concealed).

The turn comes a four, five, and seven out there. The man on my immediate right is Mr. Bill Boyd, an executive at the Golden Nugget Casino in Las Vegas, and, in my opinion, the best stud player in the world (I'd rather have early frost on my peaches than play stud with Mr. Boyd, but he'll play hold'em, too). Mr. Boyd bets. I believe that, within reason, I can beat whatever he's got. But I don't want to raise him and stool my hand, so I just even up call.

Another fellow from Oklahoma City calls it. Also, a dear friend of mine from Tennessee — we call him Long Goody — calls this bet. Now this boy's a top professional player and good, and I figure him for a hand, which he doesn't tattle on, either. I think the world of Long Goody, although I must say he has been a hardship on me all my life.

The next community card turned is an ace. Well,

neighbor, that's practically a cinch hand. I've got a cinch hand unless one of these cats has a six and eight in the hole. My thinking is that Mr. Boyd probably has himself an ace and another seven, which would make him two pair. If this is so, I'm going to break him.

Sure enough, Bill Boyd cuts down on the pot, he bets about $1,600. I figure no need for this slim country boy to run these other folks and their money out, since I know damn well I got the best hand. So once again I just call Mr. Boyd's bet.

Another man around the table passes. It gets to Long Goody and he raises. Now it's Mr. Boyd's action, and sure enough, he's on a cold bluff — he can't beat it with nothing, and he tosses in.

But I'm trapping for Goody, and I've got him in my snare. I figure him for trips. *He's got three fives.* So I raise it, and Goody "comes to the center like we did last winter." We get all our checks in, with another card still to come.

"Whatta you got, Slim, you got a hand?" Goody asks.

It doesn't matter what's known now, so I tell him, "Yeah, I got three aces."

He admits he has three fives.

I'm feeling damn good because in this seven-handed game, fourteen cards had been dealt to players and there are four cards in the middle, a total of eighteen cards. That leaves thirty-four in the deck, only one of which would win for Long Goody — a five. It's a 33 to 1 shot that he doesn't get it.

You guessed it, neighbor. The dealer burned one and turned one, and off come that five!

It goes to show that being drawed out on can happen to anyone. That was a case of me trying to trap a man to win all of his money, and then having him spring the trap shut on me. (By the way, that boy took those winnings and went home and bought a ranch. With my compliments, I should say, because I sure as hell paid for that spread. He named it the Four-5's Ranch.)

Long Goody is a good player — he plays in the World Series of Poker every year — and he's done that same thing to me two or three times in my life. Everytime that anybody has beat me out of a good pot, I remember it. Like that time during the World Series of Poker in 1970 when we were in another hold'em game, Long Goody and me.

I have a queen of clubs and a queen of spades as my hole cards. *Long Goody has the queen of diamonds and eight of diamonds.* The turn comes and the flop consists of the queen of hearts, six of diamonds, and four of clubs.

Goody bets and I play back at him. Since I have kind of a reputation as a bluffer, he doesn't think I have a damn thing, so he calls the raise. Now I've really got him tied in this pot. (With what he's holding, he's dead in the pot right now; the only thing that could help him would be two diamonds in those last two community cards, and the odds of him getting those are about 40 to 1).

It still hurts to think about what happened. The next card off is a seven of diamonds. The last card is the king of diamonds. Goody beat me another monstrous pot when I held what I thought was a cinch hand.

That boy has held over me all his life. That's an expression that can be true in poker — there are players who always seem to make the best hand against you. I hold over certain players myself, one of them a boy in Louisiana who's a real pro player. Whatever he's got, it never is any good against me.

I've said hold'em is a game that involves a lot of luck, but it takes some skill, too, if you're going to be a winner. One little trade secret that'll benefit you, though, is take a turn, in position, with any two-suited cards that are close together. I'm not advising to stay in any monstrous pot with say, an ace and six of diamonds, because there's just one kind of good hand you can make with that — a flush.

But, for instance, if you have the ace and jack of diamonds, then stand a raise, a good raise. Why? Because you can make a straight or a flush; you could even make four jacks or four aces with your hand. But with that ace, six I spoke of earlier, you can't draw a straight; you couldn't with an ace, seven; ace, eight; or ace, nine. However, if I've got the ace, four of hearts, I'm coming in for the turn because it might come a deuce, trey out there, the pot could be checked, and you get a five for free on the next turn, making a straight with which you could break somebody. But always remember — and I can't stress this enough — you never have a mortal cinch on a pot until all of the cards are dealt. Let's take another case in point.

Player A has two tens in the hole. The flop on the board is ten, ten, deuce. Now four tens look like a mortal lock anytime, but in hold'em, this may not be.

The reason it isn't a cinch even with only two cards to come is because anybody sitting behind *Player A* may have two jacks, two queens, two kings or two aces, in the hole, and they could make a set of fours — any of which would beat *Player A's* quad tens.

However, if I was one of those players and holding two jacks, and the turn comes up a ten, ten, deuce, I'd give another man credit for having a ten. Four tens, no. But I'd likely get loose of my hand without losing any big amount of checks. By the same token, if you happen to be *Player A* with those four tens, don't start playing too hard and tattle-taling your hand. You've got one of those concealed buggers where you're looking for somebody who's drawing at a flush, or somebody who's come in the pot with a pair of concealed aces, kings, queens, or jacks.

Instead of coming in like a wildcat gusher, check those four tens. If the pot's been raised going in — and it's a cinch that it has — that cat with the two aces won't pay much attention to those two tens on the board. Even if he's thinking somebody has trips, he'll bet his hidden aces. When he does and it gets back to you, just call him — don't reveal your hand yet.

The next card off — it makes no difference what it is — check. You've got no reason to bet at this point. If you do, Mr. Two-Aces is going to think you have one of those tens. But if he bets again — and he will — play back at him now. If he has bet you twice and you've called him both times, he's committed himself to going all the way with this pot. Play back at him and you're going to break that boy. That's trapping with a hand when the trap works for you. You've got that feller in about the same spot as that Texas Aggie coyote that got caught in a trap, chewed three of his legs off and still was in it.

I want to emphasize the importance of watching the board — the up cards that make up the flop — especially when you first start playing hold'em. There're some good reasons for this. Since the community cards are played by everyone in the game, it's possible for somebody to hold the same hand that you do — but with a higher kicker. Take this situation, for instance: Two pair is a very common hand in hold'em. Let's suppose that *Player A* has two sixes in the hole. That's a turning hand, because there's a damn good chance he'll get one more to make trips, and he's going to get three cards in the flop instead of one at a time to see if he can get that other six.

The turn comes an eight, eight, and deuce. Now *Player A* has sixes and eights. Right now, he's a favorite over an ace, king because there are only two more cards to come, and a player with an ace, king must catch one of those cards to beat *Player A's* hand.

The next card off is a ten. *Player A* still holds the best hand. *Player B* has an ace, king. His hand, then, is two eights, with an ace, king, ten.

The final community card is a ten, and, as a result, *Player A* can't beat anything. *Player B* has tens and eights with an ace kicker. Since only five of the seven cards are played to make a hand, *Player A* has eights and tens with a six kicker. Actually, he's ended up with three pair which aren't worth a damn. If that last ten hadn't hit, *Player A* would have had a hand, but *Player B*, who didn't have anything to start with, wins that pot on the basis of his ace kicker.

Another major point to keep in mind is that straights and flushes are the strong hands in hold'em. My theory is that if you make one-half of the straights you draw at in one night, you're going to be a winner in the game; and if you make one out of three flush draws, you'll come out ahead. With this in mind, I'll take a turn in hold'em if I'm holding the four and six of hearts, knowing at the time that this is the worst hand. But I figure I might make a straight or flush and have a concealed hand to trap somebody with after the turn. I won't call a big raise with this hand, the four and six of hearts, but I'll call a pretty good-sized one if I'm last in position and if as many as three people have come in ahead of me. Then, if the five and seven hits on the board, I've got some kind of hand — four, five, six, seven, and two cards to come. If the flop is ten, eight of hearts and deuce of spades, I've still got a hand; all the hearts left in the deck will make me a flush.

Take a turn with any two connecting cards because of the straight and flush possibilities. I'll draw at a flush and take a chance on winning the pot whether I make it or not. My reasoning is this: If I'm drawing at a flush and a man leads off and makes me a bet, I'll always play back because of my flush draw that'll be a sure hand if I hit. Although I don't have anything at this point — not even a pair — I have a good chance of making my flush. It'll be a cinch because I'm trying for the nut (ace-high) flush since I'm holding the ace of the suit. If I play back now and he calls and I *do* flush, I damn sure won't have to worry about getting it paid off. The chips will already be in the pot.

But if I just even up call this man, and the next card off makes my nut flush, he's going to check his hand, thinking that I might have been drawing at a flush. If I play back at him when he bets, and he doesn't call, then I win a pot without even having to draw. If he calls the raise, I'm still not a big underdog, unless he's holding trips; and at the same time, by raising the pot, I'm eliminating the chance of not getting paid off by a good pot if I make my flush.

Salesmanship! That's the name of the game in poker. I'm trying to sell a man a bill of goods when I play back at him. I don't have anything except a draw and guts, but if I make my hand, his chips will be in there and I'll win 'em.

I'm not so strong on doing this with a draw at a straight. For one thing, there's a different price in making a straight than flush, although it's less than 12½ percent difference. Still, I'd like to play anything in the world in which I have a 12½ percent advantage. There are nine cards that'll make a flush for you, and there are only eight that'll make a straight, if you're drawing at an open-ended straight with two cards to come. I like that 12½ percent going for me, so I'm partial to the flush draw.

One last word on straights. I don't see any reason for you to lead off and bet on a straight if you turn one. As I've said before, you've got a trapping hand — you know you've got a cinch. If somebody takes off after you and there isn't a flush draw on the board, I wouldn't play back at him with this straight. You've already got him, and it doesn't make any difference what hits out there in the middle. The important thing to do is keep him guessing: That's the nitty gritty of hold'em, or any poker game.

Five-Card Lowball Draw

BESIDES HOLD'EM, I've played more lowball than any other game, because lowball and hold'em have replaced stud and draw with the professional poker players. Stud was the first poker game that gamblers played; and later came draw, jacks or better; but jacks or better got to be a boring game, and the card players speeded it up and called it high draw, a game in which you could stand pat with nothing or open with nothing.

That really opened new fields of poker, and I, for one, am glad that it happened because it has benefited the younger players. We can beat the old-timers who are tight players, playing these new games where there's action and so many concealed hands.

When high pass-out began to pass out, players could see that there were many more possible hands to make by playing the worst possible card combinations instead of the best ones, and that's how lowball was born. Lowball caught on fast all over the world. There are three kinds of lowball; which one you play depends largely on where you play it. The three lowball games are:

(1) *Wheel lowball*. The wheel, that's a bicycle. The best possible hand in this game is ace, deuce, trey, four, five, the wheel.

(2) *Six-four lowball*. Ace, deuce, trey, four, six is the best hand. (The only difference between wheel lowball and six-four lowball is that straights and flushes count against you in six-four and they don't in wheel.)

(3) *Deuce-to-the-seven lowball*. This is the most popular form of lowball played in the South. In this game, the ace is played high, and either a straight or a flush count against you. The best hand in deuce-to-the-seven is deuce, trey, four, five, seven.

Right now, I believe that wheel lowball is being played more frequently than the other types, so I will concentrate on it here.

Position Dictates Your Play: Bearing in mind that neither a straight nor a flush count against you in wheel lowball, it's obvious that a draw at a three, four, five, six, blank is a million-dollar hand, since the object of the game is to get the lowest possible hand. In lowball, as in any other kind of poker, position is of prime importance when you're deciding how to play your hand. Who acts first and who acts last after the deal makes all the difference.

If you're immediately to the dealer's left, you're first player to speak. Now anybody who plays poker knows that if you've got a wheel — ace, deuce, trey, four, five — open with it, and if you get any business, you've got a cinch. But you shouldn't play back (raise with it) before the draw: Let the people around the table draw, so that if they do catch a hand, they can go broke. Don't scare them out right away.

Drawing at a Ten: If you're holding an ace, deuce, trey, four, ten, naturally you open. What you do with this hand depends on how many players come into the pot; if you happen to get four players, or even three, in the pot, go ahead and draw one card to this ten, because you damn sure stand to improve your hand. You can catch, on that draw, a five, six, seven, eight, or nine. That's twenty winning cards, or almost forty percent of the deck, in your favor, to improve that ten.

If the pot is raised, you should call it and draw one card; you must draw at this stage of the game. So sup-pose you open with this hand, the next man calls, the feller after him calls and then the next player raises it. Goddamn, *call* that raise, because you're drawing at what will be a cinch hand if you make it — the wheel. But don't play back at that raise; your hand is no good at this point, before the draw. Yet, the toughest you can run into with that raiser will be a pat hand; probably the worst hand that that man could be holding is a ten high with peewees (very small cards), the same as you. And it's natural that he would raise it, trying for a one-card draw at a cinch himself. So don't play back at that raise, just call. You'll get these other two people between you and the raiser in there, too.

Okay, after the draw let's assume that you catch a nine. The two players between each take one card and the raiser stands pat. That's a good indication the pat player damn sure has your nine beat, and, even if he doesn't, you can be sure those other two men didn't call a raise to draw at a nine: so watch out for them; you've got no reason in the world to lead off and bet your nine.*

*For the chances of winning with a nine-high, pat hand, see Chapter 3.

Just pass; and if either of those other players bet, throw your hand away, because it isn't any good, neighbor. I don't care if this *No. 2* man leads off and bluffs at it, because if the third man passes and that pat player calls *No. 2*, you can figure Mr. Pat for having a hand: If you stop and think, he isn't going to call with a ten, and a ten is all that you can beat with your nine. So duck that hand fast.

Lead with a Seven: But now let's say that in this draw you caught a seven, so you're first. The next two players each take one card and the third guy stays pat. I say you should lead with that seven, because if this cat on your immediate left makes a nine, he isn't going to call you; in fact, even if he makes an eight, seven, he shouldn't call you.

But if he makes a "hellacious" hand on his one-card draw, he's got to raise you. Now you're liable to save all your money by having led with your seven and forcing that *No. 2* man to act. Lead with your seven, remembering that you've got an ace, deuce, trey, four as your other cards — a seven-four hand. If *No. 2* and *No. 3* pass, and this *No. 4* pat hand has a seven, you're going to win his checks. Even if he's got a baby eight, he's going to call you, and by doing that he'll make this hand pay off for you.

Also, by leading off, you won't jeopardize all your checks in a no-limit game. After you bet, you guess whether that seven is any good or not. For instance, if the player on your left makes a big bet, the next man passes, and the guy with the pat hand just calls, you know you've got the pat hand beat. If Mr. Pat had something better than your seven, he'd raise instead of call.

95

But hell, there isn't anything but a six or a bicycle under your hand. So, lead off with any seven.

Even if you have ace, deuce, trey, *six* and then catch a seven, go ahead and play it. If it's beaten you're going to lose anyway, because nobody's so good that he can't play a seven-six in lowball; and if it's not beaten, you'll get it paid off nicely. That man who stood pat with an eight is not going to bet it after three one-card draws around the table, because if he bets it and gets any business, he knows his hand isn't any good.

If it's down to two-handed — just you and that guy who has the pat hand — and you make a seven, I say really lay some lash to it. This goes for limit or no-limit playing. In no-limit, if he can beat your seven you're going to lose a lot of checks anyway. If he's holding something that can't beat the seven, and you lead off and bet him, you'll get a call if he's got an eight or a seven of any description. But if you *check* it, and he's got an eight-seven or something, here's where poker is really played, man. He's got no reason now to bet that eight-seven at you. He'll just show it down; because if he bets that eight-seven and gets called anywhere, his hand isn't any good. Good players don't play eight-sevens really fast after the draw (although they do to some extent in two-handed).

Playing a Snowball: A snow hand, also called a bust, frequently occurs in lowball. So here's an important rule: You never play a snowball from the front position, because of the chance of getting raised further around the table. If you get played back at, you've got to duck it and give away that money you've put out there. However, it's a different situation if you're toward the back. If three people come in ahead of you and you're next, now you can call them and play back at them with a snowball. If they've got something like a one-card draw at a nine, they're going to pass. But if they've got a one-card draw at a seven, they'll probably call you, which is all right. The next man, if he's got a pat ten, will probably chuck his hand and give up his money. Meanwhile, the man who is drawing at that seven has 3 to 1 odds against him that he doesn't make it. So I say, always play a snowball from behind.

When that man looking for a seven draws and checks it to you, bet him. I don't care if you're standing pat on two kings and a nine; it doesn't make any difference what your snow is, but of course, the best snowball to play is a little bitty one. By that, I mean if you've got two deuces, two fours, and a six in your hand when playing short-handed poker, that's a pretty good lowball hand. Now everybody says, "Why, that's nothing," and that's the truth; but if you'll stop and think for a minute and do a little mental arithmetic, it's pretty damn hard for that other player to have any little cards with you holding two deuces and two fours and a six. If he comes in and draws one, all the peewees are gone. He's liable to catch a nine, and if he does, he'll check it. That's the time for you to lay the lash to him, and make a good, big bet.

Make any Bluff a Big One: Anytime you run a bluff, it should be a big one. Don't bluff a piddling amount where some player will say, "Well, maybe he's got it and maybe he ain't." Lay enough of your chips out there to make him think a long time before he matches them. Then he'll throw that nine away.

97

Don't Raise and Draw to Anything Above an Eight: That's nothing — it's a tourist play. I don't care if I've got an ace, deuce, trey, nine, that's plainly not a hand when you're in one of those front seats. By the same token, if I've got an ace, deuce, trey, nine, queen, and I'm around toward the back end, with as many as two people coming in ahead of me, I'm coming in because sometimes — contrary to what other experts might say — you've got to draw two cards to play in lowball.

In lowball poker, people say there aren't many two-card draws, and that's the truth. But the reason for that is their position; you can't come in early with a two-card draw because if you get raised a pile of money, you're forfeiting the money you've put into the pot. You either forfeit it, or send the rest of your good money after that which you've already burned up, and I say don't do it. In other words, try to play so that if you come in with something and get it raised, you can come on and protect your money; you can call and draw at your hand. If you miss it, you can save the rest of your checks.

A two-card draw isn't so bad a play. If you do connect, you'll hear people say, "Well, lookee here, he drew two cards and beat this nine for me." Throw your chest out, because it's unusual to beat that nine with a two-card draw. Still, in about one pot out of every five, a two-card draw will do just that — beat a nine.

Lowball Action In Alabama

Alabama is where the lowball action is, and there is a group of us that meets there on occasion for this purpose. In this particular game I'm going to tell you about, people came from all over the country to play. They are all professional players, so it goes without saying that generally, these games last longer than ordinary games, and there's nothing soft in these kinds of games. You're really looking at the card talent of the world when the poker stakes get this high and these fellows sit down at the table. My reason for being here is that occasionally everybody agrees to change the game from lowball to hold'em, and when that happens, I immediately become a favorite.

We're playing seven-handed at a club — I won't mention the town or city — but it's in Alabama. It's winter, and cold and damp outside, but not inside the club, where the high action alone could keep things heated up. The game's been going on for a good spell. During the course of play, I've had three seven-hands beaten, which is a hell of a hand to get beaten in lowball. This last time, I lose with a seven-six pat, and all my chips are gone. I start making so many trips to Western Union to renew my bank roll that they know me a block away; after a while, it reaches a point where the Western Union clerk greets me with, "Here it is, Mr. Preston." In fact, I've hot-footed it down to Western Union about five times during this game. These guys around the table are really scratching me up.

Among them are such top-notch players as my old friend Johnny Moss from Odessa, Texas, who was the 1970 winner of the World Series of Poker at Las Vegas; and old Long Goody, bless him, the boy from Tennessee who's always causing me some hardship in poker. Goody hangs over my head like that black cloud over that little guy in the L'il Abner comic strip, Joe Something-Or-Other.

At one point during this Alabama game I draw at a seven and make it, and another man draws at a seven and makes his, too. I've got a seven, five, four, deuce, ace; while he's got a seven, five, trey, deuce, ace. That four costs me the pot. Goddamn, it was one of those hands where if you're beaten, you've got to go broke. Anybody who plays well enough not to go broke with a seven in lowball plays too damn well for me!

I decide then that it's time for me to walk around a little. I'm slicker than a wet gut (I've lost all my money), so I decide on getting me some rest. I go to my room and sleep for about six hours; that's what I like to do when I've played a marathon session — not sleep a long period of time right off. I get up and get me some grub and then go sit through a movie, and after that, I return to the room and sleep ten hours more. Yet this doesn't slow the game down at all. There were plenty of players around, and as soon as I got up, someone either took my seat, or else they continued to play six-handed until somebody else joined the action. Feeling just fine after the sleep, I go back to Western Union and get a new bank roll, and return to the game.

I'm in a hand and I get a queen, deuce, trey, five, six — a one-card draw at a six-high. I'm in front and I open it, and then it gets around to Long Goody, who's got some sort of hand. Naturally, I don't know what he's got, but he shoots the pot up.

It comes around to The Captain, a grizzled, old retired river boat captain, and he falls in there on top of it. This tells me that The Captain is drawing: I know that with a pat hand, he'd have played back instead of just calling. I've got lots of checks in front of me, so with my deuce, trey, five, six draw, I call Goody's raise. The minute I call him, that ends the betting. Now there are three of us in a pot that a show dog could jump over. I'd won a very big pot just before this hand, and these other boys are also winners in the game, so this game is getting out of shape. This is about the fourth or fifth day that it's been running.

I draw and catch an ace, which is exactly what I was looking for. I look down and see this ace, deuce, trey, five, six, which makes me a six-five hand, and I say, "How sweet it is!"

Mr. Goody is no disappointment to me, either; he stands pat. The Captain draws one card, and I figure he's drawing at a seven or six-high, or maybe even a wheel. Since I've made my hand, it'll take a wheel or a six-four to beat it.

I'm first and I lead off the betting pretty high. The boy on my left stalls and stalls, and I think, "Well, now, this cat's got him a hand." But I don't know whether he's trying to stall The Captain into the pot, or play back at me. However, he disappoints me a little and finally throws in his hand. Then it gets around to The Captain; *he's caught himself an eight-high.* Now my reputation is such that when the pot gets big enough, I'm liable to bet big whether I've got a hand or not.

Being aware of this, I'm sure that The Captain is thinking "Well, ol' Slim has caught himself a king, and maybe he's thinking that Goody didn't have a good hand, and that I might pair something." After giving it due consideration, The Captain comes in on top of me. Well, I win a monstrous big pot with that six. A quick glance at my checks (I never count them while I'm playing), shows that for the whole trip now, I'm not in too bad shape, even with those Western Union trots that I've had to make.

We rock along, and about eight or ten hours later,

I get jammed into a pot. Somebody has opened it about two seats in front of me, and the next man has called it, and I've got a nine, six, five, deuce, ace — a pat hand. Since there's been no speed shown to this pot, I shoot it up. I lay the quirt to it. But now the game's gotten out of shape, the way they always do when they run this long.

After I had won this other good pot, Mr. Goody had gone and taken himself a little siesta, and now he's back in his seat. It gets to him and he falls in on top of this, which tells me something: This boy's really a professional player. He knows that two people already have come in this pot, and that I'd raised it. Although, those other two players could have a better hand than me, and there's no telling what I've got, Goody still falls in on top of me.

It gets around to the two players who came in ahead of me. The first man calls, and the second raises. I can see now that my nine-six, in all probability, isn't any good. I've got two choices: I can gnaw loose from the damned thing, or I can come on in and draw one card at the six. I decide to call the raise, and so does Goody.

Now the first man, who happens to be Mr. Johnny Moss, raps pat. I assume my nine isn't any good, so I discard it and draw a card; Goody also draws one. Damned if I don't catch right back on that nine.

Johnny, who had the pat hand, passes. When he does this after Goody takes one card, I do some quick figuring: There were four of us started in this pot, so I know that's as good as sixteen low cards gone. These other cats sure as hell didn't come in with tens, jacks, queens, kings, or probably even nines, like some damn fools. But there's so much money riding on this pot that after Goody draws his one card, I decide to go with this nine, knowing there aren't many peewees to be drawn at.

If Goody has caught him a nine, he'll probably throw in; even if he catches an eight, he may duck it. I decide to bluff with my nine; although it isn't altogether a bluff. A nine *could* win, but I know it hasn't much chance. I consider it a bluff because if I get called, I know I'm beat.

I move in on Goody, making a big bluff. I reach to the back and pull up some slack and slide to the center. Mr. Goody stalls a while, and then throws in his hand. Now I think I'm pretty safe with this nine. I figure that Johnny, the other guy left in the pot, has an eight-seven pat; and if that's so, he's going to throw it away after the bluff I laid on. But Johnny Moss is no ordinary player. That clever old Mr. Moss is sitting there with a fabulous hand. *He is pat with a six-four!*

When I drew my one card, I was drawing dead in the pot even then. Even if I'd caught a trey, which would have been a perfect card for me, or a four, I'd still had a six-five and lost the money.

Well, I felt badly enough about it, and that slicked me off again. I decide that's about the tail end of my playing down here in Alabama, so I get up, put on my overcoat, and head for the door.

Everybody's hollering things like "Slim, are you through? Are you gonna go and leave this money here, or get you some more money and try to win?"

I'm damn sure through with it, though. I tell them "You can damn sure stick a fork in me because I'm done. I've enjoyed just about as much of this as I can stand."

Johnny Moss and I have been friends for a long time, and he has the courtesy to get up from the table and come talk to me — because he has just won all my money.

He says, kind of worried, "Slim, where you going?"

I already have the door open, and the cold wind was

103

whooshing through, but I turn and tell him, "No one knows where the hobo goes when it snows." And I walk out. That remark has been attributed to me and has stuck all the rest of the years since that game . . . .

Well, it should be obvious to anybody from all that money I lost that Mr. Johnny Moss did the right thing with his hand in that Alabama lowball game. He had a big hand and he didn't let on that he had anything, and so I broke myself in that situation. I came off that nine and then came back on it when I drew; and when Johnny checked it, he trapped me.

This is just another damn good example of the benefits of not playing a pat hand before the draw. When you're playing lowball, give everybody a chance to get in and either make a hand that you can beat, or, as in my case, give a fool like me a chance to come in and make something and bluff at it. But start with some kind of hand: This is especially true in limit poker. In any game that's played with a limit, the element of bluff is practically eliminated, although not completely. If a player shows a lot of weakness to you, then go right ahead and take his checks, if you can, with a bluff. Generally, however, my advice to anyone playing in a limit poker game is don't bluff. You haven't got a dog's chance with a bluff because it only costs a nominal fee to call you.

Most of the so-called experts say that you can't draw two cards playing lowball, but I believe that's old-fashioned. Nowadays, the ante has been graduated in these poker games. If you sit there and wait for a pat hand or for a one-card draw, why you're apt to have moss all over your seat before you come into a pot. *I* say that if you've got a solid two-card draw, give it a try now and then. I'm *not* saying draw to an eight, though. If you've got an eight in your hand and still have to draw two cards. You're like that polar bear — you're on a cold-ass trail. You don't have a chance to win with that hand; but say you're holding ace, deuce, trey; ace, deuce, six; or six, five, four. Come in and draw two cards if you're in the tail-end position.

Of course, you've got to realize you've got the worst hand on a two-card draw. Yet, if you hit, you're more apt to get the hand paid off, since everyone around the table is snickering, "Well, he drew two cards." And I say you're entitled to win some money off a man if you draw two cards and beat him out.

Your chances of being pat with a good hand are not high in a game. You probably won't hold five pat hands in a twelve-hour session or even in a four-hour get-together. And you probably won't have twenty, one-card draws during this same period. So, if you're giving up your ante all the time, you'd better try to get some kind of two-card draw and come into some of those pots. You sure as hell can't win anything unless you get in.

One thing is for certain in a lowball limit game: You can't play a snowball — that is, a bust hand. Suppose you have a snow hand, and another player draws one card and catches a ten. He passes, and you try to take his money bluffing with a snowball. By this time, the pot's so big that he's going to come to whatever your limit is on the game; he'll call your one extra bet on the suspicion that you're playing some kind of a snow. So anytime you're tempted to try to run one with a snowball, just remember that old adage of mine, partner: "No one knows where the hobo goes when it snows." And you won't go broke.

8
Five-Card Stud

I THINK STUD poker is a game of the past, not only in America but just about anywhere in the world — it's as plain out of style as hoop skirts, ten-cent hamburgers, and passenger trains — and there aren't really any big stud games left in America or England. In the gambling state of Nevada, I'd say there might be one stud game to 10,000 other poker games, and there's very little stud played in the house games. In my opinion, there's just no excitement to stud — it's a dull, lifeless game. I won't play it with the professionals, although I can take care of myself in the average stud game — if I don't go to sleep.

But if you *are* in an area where stud is played, I can give you some pointers that'll make you a winner in those hometown games. I should warn you in advance that I'm not in agreement with the stud strategy that has become practically poker scripture, just because some expert who wrote a book said it was so. Through the years, I've read some of the books that have been written about poker, and I thoroughly disagree with a lot of the authors' advice on stud poker. Frequently, if you play stud the way some experts have recommended, you might as well be playing with a deck of marked cards. Your style will be so silly that a six-year-old kid could figure it out.

Everyone knows that the best possible starting hand you can have in stud is two aces backed up. But if you will not come into a pot unless you have a ten, jack, queen, king or ace in the hole, anybody can play with you for a few hands and know exactly what you've got. It's more obvious than a marked deck if you are waiting for the big cards to come before you act.

In a ring stud game, if my up card is comparable to the up card of anyone around the table, and if I've got anything from a seven on up in the hole, I'll take the next turn whether I'm paired or not. I'm not saying that I'll take a queen and a seven and go after a man who has an ace up, because I know I've got the worst of that.

Recently I read a poker book by a fellow who said that if he had two deuces, treys, fours, fives, sixes, sevens, or eights in the hole, he would only take one card to this pair. I think that kind of reasoning is like when Corrigan went around the world — completely in reverse. This is why I disagree with that theory:

Suppose you've got two fives back-to-back. If there isn't another five showing in any other hand, you've got to assume that the other two fives are in the deck. If you're playing seven-handed poker, that means fourteen cards have been dealt, leaving thirty-eight cards in the deck. In figuring your price, you have two cards out of thirty-eight to catch in order to make a set of trips. Two out of thirty-eight would be odds of 18 to 1 that you don't draw one of those fives.

Why do I believe you should stay and take more than that third card? As an example, let's say that the third card you draw is a king. On the next draw, if no fives or kings have appeared on the board, you've got three kings and the same two fives to help your hand. By now, twenty-one cards have been dealt, and of the thirty-one cards left in the deck, five of them are winners for you. The odds now are only 5 to 1 that you don't catch a five or a king on that last card.

Now I don't say that you should take another card if another player has two eights or two tens or any over-pair looking at you; but if it is not certain that you're beaten, take another card, because if you catch a five, you're liable to win a monstrous pot. If you turn a king and run into somebody with a little old pair, why then you're going to knock some tail feathers out of him!

If you're going to stay in the game only on high cards, there is nothing in the world to playing stud, because when you come in you're telling everybody what you've got. If your up card is a deuce and your next card is a seven, all the players know you haven't got a pair of deuces or sevens: You've told them that by your tight playing style. If you happen to catch a queen or jack and make a bet, then you're telling them "I've got two queens or two jacks." You *must* diversify your game.

You don't have to have a ten, jack, queen, king or ace to come into a pot, although of course, anybody would love to have those backed up aces. But you've got to know how to play them, or they won't do you any good, either. If you show too much speed when that second ace lands, you're eliminating any guess as to what you've got in the hole. You sure as hell won't get any business. Unless you run up against a big hand in the first three cards, you can't get those aces paid off; it's like all the other games in this respect — with a good concealed hand, you've got to set a trap for somebody with a betting hand that isn't as good as yours.

An example of this would be if you were backed up with two sixes, and then a third six falls. Another player has an exposed pair of kings. Naturally, the man with the two kings is high and he bets. He can't afford to check and give you a free card because he figures you might make three sixes on him (which you've already done, of course). Whatever you do, *don't* raise this cat and stool your hand. He's going to bet on those two kings, and you'll win a good pot. You see, if you play back at him when he bets, you're telling him "Mister, I've got three sixes, so those two kings you've got up are no damn good."

If you've got a set of trips, don't play back at another hand in stud poker. It's goddamn hard to make a set of trips, and you better try to win some money with them while you've got them, instead of running everybody out.

Now, say that same feller has an eight in the hole, and on the next turn he catches another eight, while you catch a ten. This man will bet his two kings and eights, and if you play back at him now, he's going to think, "That boy hit his hole card with that ten, so he's got himself tens and sixes. I've made kings and eights. I'm gonna break this man."

That's the difference between losing and winning poker, neighbor. If you had played back at him with those three sixes at the start, he would have ducked his two kings. Now, instead of winning his one little old bet, you're going to break him, because he won't get loose from those kings and eights, which he thinks will beat your tens and sixes.

So if stud's your thing, keep these points in mind. Your chips will pile up.

Seven-Card Stud

IN THIS GAME, you're dealt two cards face down and one card face up before there's any wagering at all (the rest of the deal consists of three more up cards and one down card), and your first three cards in seven-card stud should determine what you're going do with the hand.

Draw at a Flush: You've got a hand if you're holding three cards of the same suit. Go on with this card combination to this extent: If the next card makes you a four-card flush draw, then you've got three more cards to make it. Take the full seven-card deal. If you're lucky enough to hit this flush on your seventh card, which is concealed, you'll win a bigger pot; but if you've got four diamonds face up, another man's going to give you credit for having a diamond flush, because you had to have something to start in that pot. So that "down the river" card — that's what the last face-down card is called — is the best possible one on which to make your hand.

However, if the fourth card is of a different suit than that of your first three cards, you don't have any kind of a hand. Of the three cards to come, two must be diamonds for you to win. You're pretty much an under-

114

dog, so don't take more than two cards trying to make this flush. If that fourth card doesn't at least give you a pair, and if somebody doesn't make a pretty good wager, why, use your hat for a quirt and whip your ass out of that pot! You have no business in there now.

Draw at a Straight: The same principle holds true if you're shooting at a straight. Let's say you're holding three cards in sequence, maybe six, seven, eight. Even if they're all different suits, go ahead and take off another card. However, if you catch something like a deuce to that hand, that should be the end of your drawing; because now you've got a two-card straight draw with just three cards to come, and it's unlikely that you'll be able to improve your hand.

If you're drawing at a three-card straight, it's the same as the flush draw strategy: Unless your fourth card helps or pairs you, get out. If the card makes you a pair, then take that fifth card. You may make a set of trips, or two pair, or even the straight you're shooting for. For myself, I'd rather catch that straight card than make a set of trips, because the trips will be wide open for everybody to see and you can't win a big pot that way. But if that last "down and dirty" card makes your straight, the other players are going to be a little hesitant — they'll try to guess whether that card gave you a concealed hand or not.

Incidentally, the odds for your hitting on a straight are damn good if that fourth card is in sequence. Suppose now that you've got a six, seven, eight, nine. With three draws to do it, you can just about bet all your chips that you make the straight, because there are twenty-four cards in the deck that are winners for you, if no fives or tens are exposed on the board. With three draws at the eight cards that would make your straight, don't hesitate about taking the full seven cards to that kind of a draw.

Trips to Start: As everybody knows, if your first three cards are a set of trips, then you've got the best possible starting hand in seven-card stud. So by all means, take all seven cards on that hand. It doesn't even matter what your fourth, fifth, and sixth cards are: With four cards still to be dealt, the odds are great that you'll make a full house or even a set of fours. Every time you catch a card that's not paired with any of the others showing on the board, there are three more just like it in the deck that will make you a full house. When you draw that last card, you've got ten winners in that deck that'll make you a cinch hand; you've got a shot at a full house or a set of fours.

Start with a Big Pair: If you hold any big pair in those first three cards — such as aces, kings, or queens — go for the full seven-card deal until you're obviously beaten, especially if one of those pair is down and the other up. At this point you may already have the winning hand; if you don't, the odds are in your favor for drawing the winning hand.

Of course, if you look over the table and some cat is obviously making a flush — that is, four face-up cards of the same suit are looking at you — then duck your big pair and wait for another hand.

Play a Small Pair If . . . : Ordinarily, coming into

116

a pot with a small pair is the way you lose your money in seven-card stud and in most other poker games. I'm speaking of anything from eights on down. If I've only got a small pair in those first three cards, I'll see only one more card. If that fourth card doesn't make a set of small trips, I'll duck that hand damned fast; otherwise, I might draw and make it and then go broke. Unless that fourth card two-pairs me or makes trips, I'm through with it.

There is, however, one exception: Suppose that a player has two eights in the hole and a jack face up, and his fourth card is a king, queen or ace, and none of his cards are showing anywhere else on the board. In that situation, the deck is what we call "rich," which means that there's a world of jacks, queens, kings, and aces left in it. In that case, the player should take a fifth card.

If he happens to catch an ace, he'll have two pair, and two pair — especially two high pair — is a strong hand in seven-card stud. Now don't get me wrong: Two pair won't win a real big pot; because if a big pot comes up and the betting gets out of shape, those two pair are strictly for the tourists. The other players wouldn't be in there doing that betting if they couldn't beat them. So just remember: Everything is decided on your first three cards in seven-card stud.

10
Razz (Seven-Card Lowball)

RAZZ, OR SEVEN-CARD lowball, is a popular game in some places. We have a razz tournament every year in the World Series of Poker at Las Vegas. Razz is dealt like seven-card high — two cards down and one card face up before the first betting interval, followed by three more up cards and one last down card, with betting after each turn. And again, as in seven-card high, you should determine from your first three cards how you're going to play the hand. Also, as in five-card lowball, the wheel — ace, deuce, trey, four, five — is the best hand.

With seven cards, don't start with any bad card up. You can play a snowball, or a bust hand, in razz, but if you do, you want it to be concealed.

Remember to mix up your play, so you won't be a typed player. If you're one of those guys who continually play only with the a.b.c. — that's what we call the ace, deuce, trey — as your starting cards, when you start catching small up cards, you'll look around and find that everybody else is out of the pot. So it's good to play a snow once in a while, even if you lose with it. Of course, don't lose too much with such a hand, but keep them guessing what you'll come in with and what you won't. The guessers are losers, you know.

Razz (Seven-Card Lowball)

An eight is a winning hand in seven-card lowball, and yet, while drawing at the eight, you've still got a shot at three lower notches — the seven, six, and five. Needless to say, I'd rather have my eight as a down card instead of up.

I wouldn't recommend coming in with a six, seven, eight, although you've got a chance to make that eight and win; with this hand, all you can beat is a nine, and a nine in seven-card low is a bluffing hand and hardly a hand with which to get a heap of checks in the pot. That is, unless you can see that a man's got a couple of picture cards up; then you've got him — so go all the way with that razz hand.

Take another example: If you've got an ace up and a deuce and a king in the hole and you're near the tail-end position, then come in with those cards, because that's a hand that you can misrepresent, since the big king is concealed. However, if that king is up and you come in, you'll get into a world of trouble: If two more people wind up in the pot, even though one may have a worse draw than the other, they can sandwich you. (Sandwiching is when two players get a third guy between them and start raising back and forth to the limit of raises. They're not actually partners, but they're going to take two to one on their hands by continually see-sawing those raises.) Always avoid getting into a spot where you can be sandwiched.

Of course, if you happen to be drawing to an ace, deuce, trey, four, you're willing to be sandwiched. Yet with just one card to come, you know within reason that you've got the worst of it because those other two guys figure to be pat. I'm talking about a situation where six cards already have been dealt. Of course, the sandwich twins can help their pat hands on that last card, too; if they've got something like a seven-five, they've got as much chance at making a bicycle on that last card as you do.

In razz I don't pay any attention at all to jacks, queens, or kings. It's highly unusual for any of these cards ever to be a winning hand when you show it down. For you to win with one of those damn kings, another player would have to have something as bad as three pair.

Start with a good hand. The only exception to that rule would be if you're playing in a short-handed game and the ante is big. You don't want to keep running off and leaving your antes, because during the times when you're lucky enough to catch three babies (small cards), you'll be the only one in the pot, with no chance at all to get your hand paid off. And the idea in playing poker is not only to make a hand, but to sell it after you make it: Get that hand paid off!

Razz always is played with a limit — it just has to be. I have seen only one poker game in my life where there wasn't a limit on razz. This happened at an Elks Club in Texas.

We played three or four days a week at this club, and usually we played hold'em, which suited me just fine. Then one day a guy said he was going to deal some seven-card lowball, or razz. Well, I felt I was a little bit of the underdog on this, but I went along anyway. We were playing table stakes — no limit on the game.

I catch me an ace, five, and six, another man has an ace up, and a third guy has a trey showing; and they bet about $50.

When it gets to me, I bet $3,000.

My reason for doing this is that I'm trying to break up this razz game to start with. I know it's about a dead-even gamble. They've got to have cards identical to mine or have the worst of it. They throw their hands away.

The next time it gets around to me in a hand, I bet all my money on three little cards I'm holding, which wound up this game pretty quickly. That's just an example of why razz is played with a limit. If there's a gambler sitting there, and he starts with three babies, and you've got a seven, six, deuce, he'll bet you all your money. It's still a drawing contest, and the gambler has not necessarily got the best of it with four cards to come. He'd actually be better off waiting until there was just one more card to draw before he bets all your money — but I wouldn't wait.

My idea is that when you've got that other fellow beat with the cards you're both holding at the moment, bet all your chips. You're liable to catch a king in the next card to fall, and he may get an eight. Now he's got the best hand, and if he bets all his chips, you're an underdog; whereas with three cards on the table you're a favorite, and with four you become an underdog.

My theory is that you should start with any three cards from the eight on down. If on the fourth card you catch a queen, give up that hand right there, and don't try to catch two little cards out of the next three draws because you can see the number of people in the pot and they've got to be holding some of those small cards. So the deck is rich with big cards, and you've got as much chance of catching one of those big ones as they have of getting a little one.

The only situation in which you'd play a bad card in razz is when it's concealed. This is the only time that the element of bluff can be put to use. (That doesn't apply, of course, if you've got a jack up and another man's got a queen showing, because that jack is to the queen the same thing that a seven is to an eight. It seems that's the only reason they put jacks in a deck in lowball — to beat queens.)

Razz, incidentally, sometimes is played with more players than in other games, and this is possible because people continually are dropping out of the pot. I've seen razz games that were nine-handed, and everybody knows that nine sevens in sixty-three; yet they never run out of cards because there are just so many little cards in there that give a player a good staying hand.

There are many combinations you can start with in three cards, but I say don't come in with any combination above an eight, unless the biggest card that you have is concealed.

For example: Suppose you've got an ace, deuce, nine, and the nine is one of the hole cards. I recommend taking a card to that, but if a bad card falls, quit right there. Don't try to chase the money you've lost starting with that bad card, because you'll only lose more. You're taking the worst of it in trying to make a two-card draw.

If you start with ace, deuce, and a concealed nine, catch a four and get a lot of business, play on because no one is pat at this point. If you make this nine hand the next card off, it figures to be good right away. If you make a nine-six on that fifth card and some man over there's drawing at a six, he'll call you. But you're still drawing at a six yourself. You've already got a nine made and you're drawing at a six, and, hell, you've got as much right to make your hand as he has. And if neither one of you helps your hand, you win the pot.

Again I say all the play in razz is from three cards.

11
The Wild Ones

WILD-CARD POKER games are strictly for the tourists, as far as I'm concerned; high-stake poker players, the pros, don't play the wild games. I've probably played most of the wild games over the years when sitting in with amateurs, but I always feel as though I'm wasting my time — that the biggest share of these Heinz varieties are for the kiddies. In this chapter, I'll go over some of the more popular games, but if you want a complete run-down on baseball or spit-in-the-ocean or whatever the hell they call these poker distortions, then I suggest you get a copy of Kaptain Kappy's Kiddy Manual.

Hi-Lo Split

This is just barely in the wild game category: The high and the low hands split the pot. There is one basic secret to winning in this game: Always go for the low hand, no matter what you hold. It doesn't make any difference if your first cards are three kings; you've got the worst of it in shooting for the high hand in hi-lo split. If someone comes in there and makes just one

126

of those nickel-high straights, or an eight-high straight, or a six-high flush on you, he's going to win both the high and the low. The wheel can be played high (as a straight) or low (as a bicycle). In some games, six-four is the best low hand, and the wheel counts only as a straight.

Dr. Pepper

The wild cards are the tens, twos, and fours — a total of twelve wild cards, or nearly one-fourth of the deck. You must have nearly five of a kind to win, and they have to be awfully damned high. Five of a kind beats a straight flush in Dr. Pepper, and five aces are the best hand.

Since there are so many possible high hands with twelve wild cards, you should stay with only the following combinations: Any three wild cards; one wild card and two aces, or one wild card and two kings; any two wild cards, with three high cards; or a three-card straight flush above a jack (queen, king, ace). Straights, flushes, and full houses aren't worth a damn in this game, so duck them.

In this game, a man could start with any three wild cards and figure to beat a set of four; it's obvious that the first card he draws will make him a set of four. And with twelve wild cards running loose in there, the odds are only 3 to 1 that he doesn't make five of a kind.

I've seen people who'll catch a couple of kings and a deuce and come in the pot, but I don't think that's worth a damn. If I was going to come in with that hand, I'd throw those two kings away and draw four cards to that deuce, before I'd draw two cards to three kings. Chances are you'll make a bigger hand than you had.

Deuces Wild

I guess the most popular wild game is draw poker, deuces wild. In this game, where the four deuces are wild cards, a full house is no hand at all. The joker is played as aces, straights, and flushes. You've got no business in a game drawing at a straight or a flush, because if you make either one and get a lot of business, you stand to be beaten. But any time you catch two wild cards in the first five dealt, move in: You've still got two wild cards (deuces), plus the joker, and the possibility of catching pairs to go with the deuces.

Suppose you've got double deuces, ten, seven, eight. Throw away that ten, seven, and eight, and draw three cards. Perhaps another person would disagree with this, but I'd rather have those other two wild cards going for me, with the possibility of drawing a card larger than the ten. The odds are only 3½ to 1 that you won't catch something bigger than the ten. And if you land something bigger, you've already moved your hand up to say, three jacks, three queens, three kings, or three aces.

By the same token, if a hand comes up in which you've got seven, eight, ten, and two deuces, you've already got a straight, of course. But I think that straight is for the tourists in this game; granted, although at the end of the pot that might be the winning hand, a lot of people will stay pat on that straight, and they'll lose a lot of checks.

Naturally, if it's a straight flush, you don't throw it away. If I had the seven, eight of spades and two wild cards, I'd draw one card to that, because you've got two deuces and a joker that'll make you a straight flush, and you've got the four, five, nine, and ten of spades still in the deck. In other words, you've got an abundance of cards that'll make you a cinch hand.

If you catch a running pair, you've already got a set of fours. If you catch anything at all, you're going to make a hand that's as good as your straight, and probably even a higher one than what you started with. So there's no reason to jeopardize your money by staying with a small straight when you can draw at eleven sets of fours — from treys up to kings — and maybe even a set of fives.

When I'm playing deuces wild, and see two natural aces, I don't pay any attention to them at all, because they're nothing — that's what the fools sitting there are playing. If you want to be winner, never come in with a hand like that — having just two aces, with no wild cards, or anything else.

Three aces, of course, are a horse of a different color. You've got the other ace, plus the four wild cards and the joker, still in the deck to be drawn at. (You've got to assume those cards are in the deck in any game where you can't see the other hands face up, because that's the only way you can figure the percentages on your catching them.)

One-Eyed Jacks, Joker Wild

All the wild-card games are high draw. I play the one-eyed jack just about fifty percent as fast as I play deuces wild because there are only two wild jacks in the deck. That cuts exactly in half the probability of catching a wild card, compared to four possible wild cards in deuces wild.

Suppose you're holding two fives, a one-eyed jack, a king, and a ten; don't just keep that wild card and draw four. You should take two cards to those two fives and the one-eyed jack. There won't be as many sets of fours and fives made in this game as in deuces wild, so you've got a good hand.

Seven or Twenty-Seven

Another wild-card game that's played occasionally around the country is seven or twenty-seven. To me, however, it's no game at all, because you've either got seven or you've got nothing. In this game, each player is dealt two cards face down, after which the betting starts. From then on, the cards are all face up. After two cards are exposed, you can see whether or not a player has exceeded the seven. All picture cards count as a half, the ace can be played either as one or eleven, and all the other cards at their numerical value. So if you start with an ace, six down, you're sitting on a cinch for the pot. If you're not exactly on seven, I'd say get rid of the hand, unless you look around the board and see that everyone's face card is a seven or greater, so that you know that the best they could be playing is eight.

You can continue drawing to the hand as long as there is a bet. A lot of people who have passed seven will go on and try to make that twenty-seven, but I say that's for the suckers. There's really only one smart way to play this game, and that's to start with two small cards. If your first up card puts you over seven, then don't take any more cards — either stay pat, or give up the pot — because if you keep chasing that twenty-seven, you're liable to get scooped for both sides of it; and since the seven and the twenty-seven split the pot, the best you can get would be half the money that's in.

If you're sitting on a seven, don't let on about your hand: When people bet, just call, and if people raise, don't play back — just call — because this is another one of those cases where you've got a cinch. There's no reason to run anybody out who may want to draw. And if there are three people in the pot, you know that you're going to get half of the money from two of them when they go running up that scale, trying for twenty-seven.

But my feeling is that this game is best suited for old women and little kids.

Low Hole Card Wild and All Others Like It

I know of only one game with wild cards that's been played in high-stake poker by the pros, and that was when some boys from Tennessee thought up a game in which the low-hole card and all others like it are wild.

This is a seven-card game. If you have a deuce and a queen in the hole and a deuce up, then you've got two wild cards. However, this is a game that can backfire on you: Always keep in mind that the name of the game is low hole card wild. That final seventh card is dealt face down. Now if you start with two fives backed up, you've got two wild cards and what looks like a hell of a hand; but if that seventh card is anything *below* a five, you no longer have those two backed-up wild cards in the hole. Even a backed-up pair of queens is worth nothing, because you have to catch a king on that last card to still have two wild cards — those queens.

One thing for sure in this game: If you don't have more than one wild card, you haven't got a hand. Let's say you have a six and a queen down and your up card is a jack, and then a seven turns up as your next card. Your six is wild, and all you've got is two queens in that pot. After four cards have been dealt, you can bet a nickel to a dog turd and hold the stakes between your teeth that your hand is no good, because it's a damn cinch that somebody can beat two queens after four cards have been dealt. Personally, I'd just as soon play Old Maid as these wild-card games.

12
Poker Etiquette— Some Do's and Don'ts

ETIQUETTE MAY BE A high-faluting word for a poker player to use, but there are some do's and don'ts of conduct that are accepted more-or-less as standard behavior among poker players all over the world. Perhaps the toughest lesson in etiquette that I ever learned took place in merry England, where they really do play like gentlemen (even though the basic idea still is to take your money). It has been said that I talk a lot when I play, and that's the truth for sure; but there is a good reason why I do this. If I'm not involved in the pot, I don't talk to the players who are; but if I am a participant, I talk to the other players because I'm hunting for a weakness in their conversation or some sort of a tell that will indicate what a player is holding. Or I may just be giving those people in the pot a snow job about a hand that I don't have. So the talking is part of my poker psychology, as I've explained earlier. There were, however, two instances in my life where talking really hurt me, and both happened in a high-stake game in London.

It's a foggy day in old London town, where I'm playing in the Curzon Club. Now British poker is quite a bit stricter than ours anyway, and there is one rule that prohibits talking while you're playing your hand. There are only three things you can say when it is your turn to act: "Call," "Pass," or "Raise it" — no more, no less. If you open your mouth at the wrong time in one of these English poker games, neighbor, somebody will put his foot in it.

In this particular game, I've got one of those British cats locked up cold turkey. He makes a good bet, but I want to stall and sell him my hand because I know I've really got him.

So the dealer says to me, "It is up to you, sir."

I answer, "Just hold on a minute there, partner. I think I got me a big pair down here in this hole." I act as though I were looking at my hand to make sure of what I've got, when suddenly, they count me out of the pot.

"What the hell's going on here — I haven't passed!" I protest. And I sure as hell didn't intend to pass: I intended to vacate that boy's chair over there.

So a really smooth cat answers, "I'm sorry, sir, but that is cheating."

"Cheating? What the hell do you mean, cheating?" I demand indignantly.

This polished dude tells me that it is a "word of mouth" kind of cheating — that by talking about a big pair I may have in the hole, I'm "falsifying" my hand, and one does not falsify one's hands in London poker games.

"You cannot discuss your hand, sir," this British Emily Post says. "You may only act on your cards." He seems on the edge of being a little put out.

"Oh, my God!", I moan. But my groaning doesn't do any damned good, so I accept the ruling and give up my money — very reluctantly, I might add.

We rock along and I become interested in another

135

good hand. Before I even stop to think, when the betting comes to me I tell everybody "Uh huh! I think I got this cat. I think I'll introduce him to Mr. More," reaching for my chips to push in a big raise.

Someone shouts, "Foul! Forfeit! Forfeit the pot!"

And forfeit it I did.

That was the tail-end of my talking, too. Anyone who knew me would not have recognized old Silent Slim during the remainder of *that* game.

Those errors are good examples of why it's so important to know the rules at the start of the game you're playing in, in order to follow the accepted etiquette. You must learn to adjust to the rules of games in various places with players whom you may not know: and you must have a definite understanding about such practices as burning top cards, cutting the deck, the raise limits, the best hands, settling up, and getting a new deck if you ask for it. For instance, there are certain sections of the country where burning that top card when dealing is not practiced. In the games I play in, it is traditional to discard that top card at the start of each deal, right after the cut.

Another etiquette "do" that I think is important is to always shuffle the cards face down. Being a hawk-eyed bastard, I can see a card if it has just been flashed, and anytime I can see a card, it's beneficial to me — whether that card concerns my hand or not. It will have to concern someone's hand later, so I take advantage of any card that is exposed to me.

Regarding the question of cutting the cards, I believe that it should be a plain and simple one-handed cut by the player immediately to the dealer's right. A one-handed cut always is best, because that way, there cannot be any hocus-pocus. If I were in a game and a player

were cutting those cards two or three times with both
hands, I'd be pretty wary of that cat, because he's either
locating some cards on you, or else he's got some strippers down in that deck, and he's trying to pull certain
cards to the top or to take them out of play.

However, logical as the cutting procedure I've described is, game rules concerning the cutting of the cards
will vary around the country. For instance, sometimes
right in the middle of a pot, somebody will say, "I wanna
cut the cards! Lemme cut the cards!" Well, that's all
right, but in high-stake poker games, we don't play by
that kind of rule. Except at the start of the deal, the
only time that you can cut the cards in these high games
is when a card is accidentally exposed. And the person
calling for the cut cannot cut them unless he is to the
immediate right of the dealer. The cutter is *always*
the player to the dealer's right. You have probably played
in games where Old So-and-So sitting way over there
wants to cut the deck. Don't hand the deck over there
— that just isn't proper — hand it to the person behind
you for the cut, the player to your right.

Poker players shouldn't get into that bad habit of
wanting to "cut the cards, cut the cards, cut the cards."
People say that a cut dog has no pups, and that's the
damn truth. That kind of cutting the cards every time
you turn around is for people either hunting luck with
their ass, or trying to cut off something with their hands;
and all it does is slow down the game and cause everyone
to want to cut the cards. It's always the same price in
a poker deal. I don't care if you flip a coin four times
in a row and it turns up heads every time — it's still
an even chance that it will come up heads the next time.
But a lot of people still keep yelling "cut! cut! cut!"
trying to outguess the cards, when all they're doing

really is tattle-taling their hand. If some player asks for a cut before drawing one card, every poker player there knows he is trying to cut them off to make a flush; it is very stupid to ask to cut the cards in that situation.

Another question of etiquette that comes up frequently at a poker game is seating position — a player's location in relation to the dealer. Any good player wants the best seating position he can get, of course, especially if he knows the playing habits of the others in the game. For example, nobody wants to be to the immediate left of a fast player, like me, mainly because of my habit of raising a lot of pots, with the idea of getting people off guard and trapping them when I do make a big hand. The only fair way to handle this problem in any game is to draw cards for seating position. And whoever is unfortunate enough to draw that hot spot must sit there.

Arguments over what is the best hand also come up more frequently in poker games than you'd think. For instance, some people consider that four-of-a-kind beats a straight flush, whereas I say that a straight flush is the winning hand over a set of four.

These arguments break out particularly when you're playing wild-card games. Perhaps somebody will want to know whether a set of five beats a straight flush; I've played in games in which a set of five was considered the best hand, while at other poker sessions, the straight flush was the top hand. I favor the straight flush winning over the five-of-a-kind. So it is certainly important to have a complete understanding about these hands at the very beginning, *before* the situations come up.

A player always should be careful not to expose his cards, whether or not he is involved in a pot. If you quit a hand, throw your cards face down in the discards because if just one of them is shown, it could benefit another player still in that pot. Suppose a player has two queens in his hand and you accidentally flash a queen as you throw in: Knowing that one of his queens is gone, it is likely that he will fold now. Or say somebody has some kind of a flush draw, and you have two cards of his flush suit in your discards: If he sees them, he knows that instead of figuring his hand with nine winners in the deck, he now has only seven he can count on, and if it is seven instead of nine, why hell, that's nearly twenty percent the worst of it.

So don't let anybody see the cards — when you're shuffling, dealing, playing, or discarding. If you don't get a good face-down shuffle when you're mixing them up, cut those cards four or five times yourself. Just whack them off, and then hand them to the man behind you to cut one more time.

Another rule to observe is *never* rib a loser when you're playing poker: That is something that is definitely frowned on. You can laugh and joke and tease with everybody, but if old So-and-So over there is losing his money, it's good fetching to let up on him. He's feeling bad enough anyway. Go ahead and beat hell out of him, but don't rib him after you do it.

And never criticize another man's way of playing his hand. For instance, I don't like to be in a game with a tight player — an ultra-conservative type who's waiting for the best hand before he gets into a pot — but I'll never openly criticize such a player. I believe that a man who buys his checks is entitled to play them any damn way he wants to. (Besides that, I'll take a tight player's money the first chance I get.)

Then, of, course there is your own conduct to be considered if you are a loser in a game. You've seen people who get mad as hell, tear up or throw the cards (or throw a little dog like The Lawyer did that time I beat him). Those kinds of tantrums are definitely a no-no. I've never torn up a deck of cards in my life, and I don't believe in squeaking if you lose.

In my many years of poker playing, I have never asked for a deck to be changed, if the deck was all right. Of course, I've been in some games where the cards damn sure needed changing, when some cat over there might be bending the cards a little, or putting a little weight on them, or scratching the pasteboards up a little. I don't say too much about that kind of conduct — I live my own life in a poker game — but that card doctoring will surely help me as much as it will help the thief doing it.

But even if it's just that you're having a run of bad luck and for that reason you want a new deck of cards, you are entitled to one if you ask for it. Everybody sitting there is entitled to change the deck anytime he wants to. Now I am not saying that it helps to switch to a new deck when you're not having any luck with the present deck; I just don't pay any attention to bad runs, because you make your own bad runs in poker.

As for the settling up in a poker game, that's something that always should be mountain-air clear before a game starts. I have to know how we are going to settle up before I get into any game; the only time I'm not interested in the settling-up procedure is when we're playing strictly for cash. (Of course, due to the numerous hijacks across America — and I'm speaking of poker games, not jetliners — we've stopped playing for cash in the big games because you get mighty tired of looking down those sawed-off shotgun barrels.)

Settling up is done differently in various places: it

might be before the game, or after the game, or before next week's game. But be certain that it is definitely established *before* you take a hand. This avoids arguments and hurt feelings that may come up when one man is a big loser and another guy is sitting there wondering how he is going to collect the money he has won. I want to be sure that the money I'm playing for is there, if I win it. If a man says he'll give me his check, I would rather *not* have his check; it's better just to wait until the next day for the bank to open, and do our playing then.

I've been in predicaments where the "etiquette," if you will call it that, was enforced; and though it may not have been to my liking, I still managed to find some advantage in it. I guess I'm kinda like that optimist who got a big box of horseshit from some joker for his birthday, and when this optimist opens it up, he's happy as hell and starts digging in all that horse dung — looking for the horse.

One incident occurred in London, when my old friend Johnny Moss and I got wind of some high-stake games. Somehow though, the news of our arrival had preceded us; and we had been checked into the London Hilton for only about four or five hours, when we had some visitors we weren't expecting.

There is a knock at the door of our room, so I open it and see two big fellows standing there, neatly dressed but with pretty tight smiles on their faces. I know right away what they are — muscle. "You must be Amarillo Slim," one of the boys says, looking me up and down.

"Yep," I answer.

"Mind if we come in a minute, Slim?" he asks, and they come right on in without waiting for an answer.

"This must be Mr. Johnny Moss," the same guy says, stopping in front of Johnny. His sidekick hasn't said anything yet.

"Yep," says Mr. Moss.

"We are glad to see you gentlemen here, and we want to welcome you," the muscle says. "Do you plan to be gambling while in our city?"

"Yeah, that's right, I am for goddamned sure," I say.

Then these two English muscle boys tell us all about ourselves — they have a lot of background, and they know that Johnny and I are ranked among the top poker players in America. At the same time, they convey their authority to us, politely pointing out that in order for us to play in London, it will be necessary that we cut in the people they represent for twenty-five percent.

Johnny, who is a small bundle of dynamite with a short-fused temper, goes through the ceiling. He cusses and tells them to go to hell while they stand there with those tight, head-breaking smiles on their faces. I interrupt Johnny's tirade. "Hey, Johnny, slow down a minute — let's see what the hell this is all about." In my own mind, I know these damn cats mean business, and though they don't carry guns in England (it is a felony), they do their work with hatchets when they get mad. Just for openers, they're liable to pin your hands to a table with hatchets.

So the muscle does some more talking, while Johnny still sputters in the background; and then they happen to mention what for me are the magic words: They guarantee that I'll get any money that I win. Now that guaranteed settling up means something to a country boy like me in a foreign land. If I'm going to play some guy who's a $10,000 man, I know he's good for it up to that ten grand, but I can't be sure of any amount over that. And I like to pull out the stops when I'm playing. If a guy loses $10,000 to me and wants to keep going in the game, that would be just fine now, because if he welshes and doesn't pay me what he owes me, I know *these* people will make it good. And he has to pay them, believe me, he has to pay them!

Looking at the overall picture, seventy-five percent of the pie looks better to me than no pie at all. You might say it's a form of insurance, my taking this deal (that I don't have any choice about anyway). I know that I won't get hurt if I go along; I know nothing will happen to me, as long as they have twenty-five percent of my take. And I know from experience that when muscle moves in, you've either got their blessing or you don't play in their territory. And if I don't take this offer and go ahead and play, I'll have some trouble — and I just wouldn't care for one of those concrete life-jackets or a hatchet wrapped around my bony old head.

I suppose muscle is a necessary evil in this business. Now don't get me wrong, neighbor. These types of people are not my associates and I don't approve of what they do. Yet, if it is convenient for me to use them to my benefit, then I love to use them.

The arrangement suited me just fine in the long run. Johnny went home, and these people put me in some games I would not have known about otherwise. There wasn't anything crooked about these games, mind you — they were on the up and up — but these people received twenty-five percent of my playing.

As far as I'm concerned, they can do their thing and I'll do mine, and it will be a peaceful co-existence. The London visit proved to be a very satisfactory one for me — and for them. I carried some of those monied bookmakers whom I played a lot farther than I would have ordinarily — I let them drown their own filly — because I knew I'd get my money.

So you see, sometimes the rules of poker etiquette require a little compromising of your usual procedures. That way, you leave good feelings behind you, you can come back and play again, and — as in my case — you're alive.

13

The Life
of a Poker-Playing Man

AN ITEM FROM the February 17, 1970, Sidney, Australia *Sun*, written by Bill Casey, called ". . . and nobody asked for swy!" reported:

The late, great Damon Runyon, once had a character, the gambler Sky Masterton, speak on the matter to Nathan Detroit.

Nathan, having had the foresight to equip himself with the answer, had challenged "The Sky" to a wager concerning the sale of Mindy's cheesecake and strudel.

"The Sky" said that his father, being a little short of anything else, had bankrolled him with the following advice. "One day a man will come along with a deck of cards, of which the seal is unbroken, and will want to bet you that the Jack of Spades will jump out of that pack and squirt soda in your ear. Do not bet him son, for you will surely finish up with an ear full of soda." Events around the sporting circles over the past week in Sidney have proved just how right Mr. Masterton was.

Half the sports around town are currently washing soda out of their ears, and boy, has it been an expensive drop.

A little over a week ago two amiable young fellows were introduced to the big boys of Sidney's sporting fraternity.

They were obviously American, as they wore ten gallon hats and spoke with a nice easy Texas drawl. They were immediately popular with members, particularly when they displayed a partiality for a small wager now and again.

"Do you play snooker?" they were asked.

"Certainly, suh, I'd be delighted," said one of the Texans.

If you happen to know anything about snooker, you probably think it is nigh on impossible for anyone to spot someone else 80 start if that someone else knows which end of the cue is for chalking.

But there is a well-known chap around town who cannot only give practically anybody 80 start, but play them left-handed, too. Supporters of this remarkable cueist now wish they had never met those Americans.

Some hours after the challenge at one of our leading clubs, their man had still not won a game, and pockets were emptied to the extent of hundreds of dollars.

Last night someone suggested a game of gin rummy, and would you believe it, one of the Texans did play a little. There are some exceptional exponents of gin rummy in Sidney, and a game was soon set up.

Thinking that it wouldn't hurt to take a little of the wind from the U.S. sails, the stakes suggested were $1,000 a game.

To the surprise of all, this was accepted with remarkable alacrity. And around six hours later, one of those ten gallon hats was filled with practically every loose dollar within reach.

I am now told that our American friends would

have trouble getting a game of marbles, even if it is a big-ring.

But they are quite willing to buy the soda . . . .

The jaunt to Sidney, Australia started like most of the fortune-prospecting journeys I make — with a rumor that some high poker was being played there. I'll go anywhere in the world for high action, especially if it is up in the six-figure bracket. Word of these games gets around; somebody will call me at home, or wherever I may be, or contact a casino in Nevada that knows where to get in touch with me.

In this case, a man phoned me and said, "Slim, they're playing some poker in Sidney, Australia, and it's supposed to be a hell of a good game. Whatta you doing?"

I was in Nevada at the time, and I wasn't very busy. It sounded like a good thing to me, so I told this boy, "Nothing, neighbor. I'd like to go down that way anyhow, because I want to buy some horses."

There was a short pause. "I don't have any money, Slim."

"You don't need any, partner," I replied. I stopped off in Amarillo just long enough to get my passport, which looks like a chicken scratched on it because of all the places I've been, and then this feller and I took a jet to Sidney. Since he was broke, I furnished the money. But we didn't know we were heading for a disappointment.

When we arrived, what we smelled cooking was not on the fire. Once again though, this big western hat and these cowboy boots of mine saved the day. I went to the race track, and I wasn't there very long before I met the kind of people I'm always looking for. Through them I found out about an exclusive club in Sidney, and I got an invitation to pay it a visit.

When I entered the club, I noticed a 6-by-12 snooker table and some tables covered with green felt, which looked downright promising. It wasn't very long before I learned they had a world-champion snooker player as a club member. They asked me if I ever played snooker; well, they didn't know it, but that was kind of like asking Howard Cosell if he ever broadcast any sporting events.

I not only cut my teeth on a pool cue in Amarillo, where I eventually became the snooker champion, but I shot snooker and hustled pool games up and down the West Coast while a young man serving in the U.S. Navy; and later, I traveled all over Europe as a civilian member of Uncle Sam's Special Services, giving pool exhibitions and chalking up with the champions of the world. This is my background, and I told these Sidney gents, "Yes, suh, I'd be delighted to try my hand at some snooker."

Well, I really dusted this champion of theirs playing snooker. Things got so exciting between him and me that the Harlem Globe-Trotters, who were playing an exhibition game in Sidney, quit at the half and came upstairs to watch our snooker game because there was no one left watching the Globe-Trotters.

After I got this snooker behind me, my partner and I were asked to join the card playing. That, of course, was what I had been waiting for, and we played gin rummy and poker, too. I went "down under" to stay ten days and ended up staying six weeks! There is a rumor that I came away with a lot of money on that trip; but what's more, I am welcome back — they even made me an honorary member of that club. The boy who went with me is not welcome back: It turns out he was a thief and a cheat, something I sure as hell didn't know when I was paying his way . . . .

Sometimes people wonder about my background, they wonder if I come from a long line of professional gamblers. Nothing could be farther from the truth. My folks were average, church-going, hard-working people. Daddy ran some cafés and a used-car business in Amarillo for many years.

I was born in Johnson, Arkansas, but my folks saw the error of their ways and came to Texas when I was less than a year old. I grew up in Texas and consider myself a dyed-in-the-wool Texan. My folks divorced when I was about eleven, and I spent part of the time with one, and then the other.

There was no gambling background at all in the family. When I was in high school in Amarillo, I used to cut sixth-period study hall with three other boys (one who became a candidate for mayor of our town in later years), and I'd go to the pool halls and bust everybody playing pool.

That's the way it all got started. First pool, and then I got interested in cards. I guess I was about sixteen years old at the time, and I was always looking for a new chance or a new way to make money. At that time, the money was important, but nowadays, money is just a toy to me — it's the thrill and the challenge of beating the best that I'm after. I don't have any set amount of money that I want to make.

As a young man, I had a keen eye and a sharp wit, and I got into games in places where other people couldn't. I started out as a pool hustler, and I became the best in my town and later played all over the country, too. I generally was "undercover" when hustling pool — I wore the cowboy hat and boots and played the role of the country kid who thinks he can shoot pool. By the time I was seventeen years old, I'd played practically all the good players in the U.S. Most of them beat me then, primarily because of my youth. But from seventeen on, I became quite proficient in pool.

I joined the Navy when I was seventeen. The Navy recruiting team had come around while I was in high school and explained that anyone who had a C average could join up and get a high school diploma. It was a good deal in the Navy: I was a captain's yeoman and chauffeur — and that wasn't a hell of a lot of work — so with all that free time, I hustled pool up and down the West Coast, using a Navy vehicle. (It definitely was against the rules and regulations, yet because of this Navy vehicle, I had gas available during the war and I had all the chow I wanted and could stay in the fine hotels for free.) It was really something: I won five Cadillac automobiles in San Francisco in one week, just playing pool — I won the Cads after winning all the surplus money that was sewed up there.

After my tour in the Navy, I thought I had all the money there was in the world — I just couldn't imagine anybody else having any left over. I had over $100,000 when I came out of the Navy. Well, it lasted me just over a year. I was still just a kid, not quite twenty.

After I went broke, this chance came along to enter the U.S. Special Services. In this job, I gave pocket billiard exhibitions throughout the European theater, and again, I had a lot of spare time over there, too. I was supposed to have been a good-will ambassador, and I guess I probably did create a little good will. But by the same token, I busted all those GI's playing poker and shooting craps and betting on the football games — making wagers on anything that was competitive.

I stayed in Special Services almost a year, just short twelve days. While I was on these tours, I played all the European champions: Erich Hagenlacher, the European balk line billiard champion, in Germany; in France, the international European three-pocket billiard champion, Roger Conti; and Joe Davis of England, the world champion snooker player. (I never beat him.)

I beat Hagenlacher at snooker because he was primarily a billiard player. I had to play billiards with Conti. I didn't know billiards and he beat me, and I told him I was tired of having him beating me playing pool. He answered, "Well, you just can't play." I told him, "I *can* play, if we lay some money on the line and if we can find a table that's got pockets on it." Before I left France, I won several thousand francs off that man because we finally went to a town where I found me a snooker table. Well, I knocked all the tail feathers out of him playing snooker, and from then on, when he and I played an exhibition game, it got a little closer. He used to beat me unmercifully, but after I broke his ass at snooker, he let up on me a little in the exhibition games.

I kept playing pool until I was about thirty years old. Yes, I've also played Minnesota Fats, first in Perth Amboy, N. J., where Fats beat me out of $12,000. Then, in 1950, he came to Amarillo and played me, and I broke him and three of his backers. I played Fats again at Atlanta, Ga., and he broke me. I have played him three times in all, and he beat me two of them. The first time Fats played me, he didn't know who I was; he beat me out of that $12,000 but he could have won five times that amount. After I left, he found out who I was and then he came to Amarillo and played me a proposition game, and I beat him — took his money and that of the three backers he brought with him.

Pool was good for me; it was very lucrative right after the war, but then it died out. The big money went to cards, so I adapted myself. My occupation is still listed on my tax returns as professional pool player, and I play in three world tournaments every year. In 1971, out of 154 players, I finished 17th. Pool was my first love, and now it's still a good sideline with me.

I thrive on the action and excitement of high-stake poker. My way of life is satisfying to me — and a man has to like his line of work. Folks have asked me why I never did "get into something else." Hell, that's a silly question, as far as I'm concerned. What should I get into — something I don't know a damned thing about — maybe building computers or inventing medical wonder-drugs or being a college professor? Would the world be better off if I made myself unhappy by opening up a shoe store or an automobile garage?

I'm not what some of the young people would call "goal oriented." I'm not looking for as much money as H. L. Hunt or Howard Hughes — I've got no specific amount I'm aiming for; money, as I've said, is just a toy to me. I'm enjoying the trip as I go along, having a good time and trying to make my family and the people I like happy, too. Most of the things in the world that I want are things that I have — how many people can say that? I enjoy gambling, and I don't hurt a soul doing it (I won't play some old boy who makes $200 a month at a service station), and there is no one who can tell me that that's the wrong way to go. If the world were to end tomorrow — of if *I* ended tomorrow — I would not regret a bit of it. Not one damn thing!

Seems like card players get all the notoriety, but how many people do you know who go to the golf course and have some kind of wager riding on it every time they tee off? It might be only a dime a hole, and yet they're as guilty of gambling as I am in any high-stake poker game. I might add I bet like hell on the golf course myself, but am I any more guilty because I bet $10,000 than some guy who bets $3? Still, they're supposed to be goody-goodies, and I'm the villain. I sure as hell don't feel that way about the life I lead.

No way around it, the life of a professional poker player *is* an interesting life. Yes, there are times when you're going to get busted flat on your ass: Nobody is always a winner, and anybody who says he is, is either a liar or doesn't play poker.

I was down South one time in a game with a bunch of the top players. One guy had lost a lot of money and he was squeaking, really squeaking. There was about six of us who went to a place to eat, while this boy was squeaking about his losses. There was no denying that he had lost a hell of a lot of money. Now most professional gamblers don't squeak when they lose, but he kept on and on. Finally, I said to him "Where'd you get that suit?"

"It's a tailor-made suit," he said.

"What'd it cost you?" I asked.

"Three hundred and fifty-nine dollars."

"What's that you're wearing on your feet, partner?" I asked.

"Those are alligator loafers."

"How much they cost ya?"

"$150."

I said, "You got on a pair of cashmere socks. What'd they set you back?"

"Six dollars a pair."

I asked him what he was paying for the suite he was occupying in the hotel.

"Forty dollars a night," he said.

"You flew down here in a jetliner, didn't you?"

He admitted that was so.

"What'd we just order now?" I asked. We were sitting at a table in a restaurant.

"Prime rib." He was beginning to look rather sheepish. Prime rib was $7.50.

I said, "All right, now lookee here, neighbor. You're wearing a $360.00 tailor-made suit, you've got on a pair of $150.00 shoes, you paid six dollars for those socks, you're staying in a $40-a-day suite, you flew here on a jet, you're eating $7.50 steak, and you're hollering? How many people do you know who do all that?"

I know I live high on the hog, but it's something you have to do when you're hunting high-stake poker. I wear both shop-made and tailor-made western suits that cost up to $550 a suit; I have a dozen or so pairs of boots, including calf, kangaroo, ostrich, anteater, lizard, alligator and nylon, that run from $225 to $1,000 a pair and up; and probably a dozen $100 ten-gallon hats. I always travel by jetliner and there is no two-week period in which I don't go somewhere by plane. I've owned a stable of race horses, but they were a liability, not an asset. I've had some ventures in the stock market that were all bad. But I'm not looking for a solid investment. My investments will be to bet on the next World Series or Super Bowl.

I do most of my globe-trotting and poker playing during the winter months, while I spend the summers with my family. We have our home in Amarillo with an Olympic-size swimming pool in the backyard, our own water well, and a flock of young ones who love to go swimming. I lead an ordinary family man's life; I've even coached Little League baseball.

My wife, Helen Elizabeth, has never played a game of chance, as far as I know. She thinks a king is the ruler of a country and a queen is his bedmate. We have three kids — the oldest boy, Bunky, is attending college on a golf scholarship; Becky, 13 , and Todd, 8, go to public schools.

My family knows that I gamble, but I keep my gambling business away from them. If I come home from a really bad trip, and I mean a *really* bad trip, and one of the kids asks, "How did you do, daddy?" my answer is the same as though it had been a mighty good trip. I tell them I did just fine, and they must think I'm the cleverest bugger in the world because I never lose. But there is no need for me to be a hardship on my family those times I do lose.

One time I was playing in Nevada and a man whom I know is with the Organization came over and asked for a piece of my play. I know these people, I won't deny it. But the extent of my association with them is "Hi" and "How are you?" They respect me because they know my word is good, that I'll do what I say I'll do. I laugh and I joke with these people, and they accept it that way. So, instead of just telling this organization feller he couldn't have a piece of my play, I told him I already had five partners. He slapped me on the back and walked off, and one of the guys sitting at the table asked, "Whatta you mean, Slim, you got five partners?"

"I damn sure do," I said, grinning. "I got a wife, three

kids and a weimaraner dog." My idea is that you catch more flies with honey than you do with vinegar. That way, you don't make enemies — and you can't afford to have those organization people for enemies.

I'm always being asked what it takes to be a professional poker player. Well, you must have a strong constitution and no nerves whatsoever. And you have to be an honest man. All the stock in trade that a gambler has is his word. Most likely, he'll have his money somewhere in a safe-deposit box, but if he needs it to meet his bets, he'll go get it or send for it. And he'll pay his gambling debts before he pays his grocery bill. And if you don't, well, it doesn't take six months in this business to find out who will and who won't. We're always running into each other — us high-stake players — wherever we go. And word gets around fast — "Old So-and-So got $2,000 from Old So-and-So, and the next time he saw him, he didn't pay him." That's the kiss-off, that feller is through in the big games because his word is no damn good.

It's a small, élite group of men who play big poker for a living. Most of them are older than me, in their sixties. But you won't find a more honest group anywhere in the world. They are tough, hard-bitten guys who have been around; they know their way anywhere on this globe, and yet, in our circle, we can lay down beside each other and sleep and leave all our money in our pants pocket and not worry about it. You can't do that with the square-johns.

In a room full of professional gamblers, we can walk off and leave all our chips on the table, even if we have to go back to the motel and change clothes, or leave the game to sleep for five or six hours. We don't worry a bit about somebody taking our chips. Now, go play in some of these private games with some of these goody two-shoes, and see how you come out if you leave your pile unattended for a minute. I've got two or three cigar boxes full of bad checks I've been given by businessmen, but I haven't got one from a professional gambler.

In our circle, when we get broke, we can borrow money in two different ways. We don't sign any notes — we don't sign anything at all. You either borrow "principle" money, or you borrow a bankroll with the understanding you'll pay it back when you can.

For "principle" money, you tell the sender *when* you are going to pay it back, and, neighbor, you pay it back exactly when you tell him. When you borrow the money without setting a repayment deadline, you may run into the lender the next day or next week in a game. But he will not ask for or expect the money until you say when you'll have it — he knows you're short, or you'd pay it back.

But principle money is just what it says, because if you are short of cash and need your money — the money you need to operate on — and you have been told a time when you'll get the money back, that's when you're supposed to get it, no later. You pay the lender principle money the following morning or whenever you can get to your stash and get your money.

And with us, there's no such thing as interest. Of course, in certain towns there are loan sharks, but I've never gotten any money from them, and I've been broke more times than I've got hairs on my head. You just don't deal with those people. If I go broke, I'll get busy and go play in some games that ordinarily I would not get into because they are small or bad games.

In this world today, nobody does any business any more without signing contracts, except professional gamblers. In the frontier days, a man's word was good enough for deals involving thousands of dollars, and it's still that way in our circle. Sometimes we go partners on a trip. Say, for instance, that Texas Dolly hears that I'm going to go on a playing trip. He may be in Fort Worth and I'm in Alaska, but he'll get on the phone and say "Slim, I've got twenty-five percent of you while you're gone." That's the way it'll be, neighbor. And when I get back, if I won $14,000, he knows I'm not going to tell him it was $8,000 and give him $2,000; and if I tell him I lost, he knows that I did — there's no question. He'll simply assume twenty-five percent of that loss. If you ever get where you can not operate that way in the gambling business, then you have no chance.

There is some gambling I will not do. I don't even know those crap tables are out there; and I won't stand playing in a poker game where they are taking money out of my pots. As I've said, I got five partners at home and I am not looking to take on any new ones, so I don't want anybody putting their hand into my pot. They can charge me by the hour — that's fine with me. In fact, that's the way I play most of my poker. Chances are that in my lifetime I've paid $20,000 in commissions for playing. That's all right because when I'm in such a game, I know what percent I am giving up — what rate per hour I'm paying.

I also will not play blackjack, because I know who has the best of it there — I know the percentages in gambling; and I know that if I play baccarat, I've got the worst of it. Now I'm not knocking these games because I'm around them all the time, but you have to be getting the worst of it when you play them, and I have to have the best of it.

I'm a winner — I play poker to win. My gambling

philosophy is that the losers walk, the winners talk. There are winners and losers, and all my life I have been a winner.

I suppose there are between eight and twelve top poker players in the United States. By top players, I mean successful players, the men who, year after year, wind up with the chips.

I think that Pug Pearson is the best all-around card player in the world. He's a winner at about any game he plays, but he's the best there is at seven-card high. Pug lives in Tennessee and Las Vegas — he recently acquired a fabulous home in Vegas. The first time I met Pug, he was a pool hustler like I was then.

Another great player is Johnny Moss of Odessa, Texas, a former World Series of Poker champion. I've played many a game with Johnny, in fact, for two or three years I saw more of him than I did my wife. Everytime I looked up, no matter where in the world I was playing, there was Johnny sitting across the table. He's been a top player for forty years, and wherever there is high action, Johnny shows up.

I would rate Bill Boyd of Las Vegas, an executive at the Golden Nugget, as the best stud player in the world. He uses a lot of psychology in his play, and he has something that is very important in poker, and that is money. If you get into one of these big games with $2,000 and another man there has $20,000, you are decidedly an underdog to start with. It doesn't matter how well you play — the big money will move in on you.

There is a man from Oklahoma City who is a top card player, George Barnes. He's another one of the old-timers. George is primarily a stud player, but he plays it all — and really well.

The Life of a Poker-Playing Man

Texas Dolly from Fort Worth has to be highly rated among the best players anywhere. Another Las Vegas card player, Jimmy Casella, is probably the best there is in razz, or seven-card lowball, but he plays all the games. He learned hold'em faster than anybody I have ever seen — learned to master it, that is.

Jack Strauss of Houston is an excellent player. He's a dangerous player in hold'em (and also a good gin rummy player). Other top-rated players are Alabama Blackie from Alabama; Addington Crandall from San Antonio, Texas, and Jolly Roger Van Osdale from Missouri. They always show up for the World Series of Poker.

There is one lady who comes to Las Vegas every year and plays in some of the high-stake games, but personally, I think a woman is meant to be loved and not to play poker. I don't think there is a top-notch woman poker player. If they happen to be doing badly in a game, they become frustrated, whereas a man seems to have less difficulty controlling his emotions. Women are tight players. They are just not "with it" as poker players, as far as I'm concerned. A woman would have a better chance of putting a wildcat in a tobacco sack than she would have of coming out to Vegas and beating me. I have played gin rummy with some women who played well, but, of course, I beat every one of them.

In my dealings, I have found that the monied people in America are the biggest phonies. With them it's all a big "I" and a little "you." These big shots want to do this and do that, but I do very little business with them, either because I know something about them, or their word is no good. It is surprising how many people are being taken regularly in some of these private games. I play in them once in a while — people will call and want me to come to their hometown and sit in a game — and it doesn't take me long to see that these people are being robbed.

But I wouldn't tattle-tale on this robber. That's his thing, and I don't bother anyone. Yet I won't stand to be robbed myself, so I have a way of letting this thief know that I am wise to what he is and to what he's doing. This is more or less a courtesy among gamblers; if I am involved in a pot, he won't take the best of it with *me*, because if he does, he has to kick my money back. I am damned sure not going to lose my money to a man knowing that he is cheating me.

A man is a fool to do something like that. For one thing, there are only so many ways that a fellow can cheat at any game, and by this time, I think I know about most of them because most of them have been tried on me. But I have a standing offer to card cheats: Buy yourself a roundtrip ticket from wherever you are to Amarillo. Then bring your money and come play me a game. And use any fool gimmick, any device, any trick you like. If you can get away with it, then you can keep what you win off me; but if I catch you, your bankroll stays in Amarillo and you use the other half of that roundtrip ticket. However, I don't know any thief who really can play. If you take away their cheating, they cannot really do anything; so when I encounter one of them, I generally cause him some bad luck.

Another occupational hazard in our business is hijacks: We get held up every once in a while. But that's just one of the hazards of this business because if we get hijacked, we don't say anything about it to the law. We're not looking to run and tell it.

Hijackers will hit the game or hit you after you leave. You are always pointed out, and they will be waiting

for you at your room, or they will come and take off
the whole game. I take some precautions, but I prefer
not to say here what they are. I've been lucky — I've
only had it about three times in the last ten years. I
missed one of the biggest ones; I was supposed to be
at that game, but I wasn't there. That is why we don't
play with cash in the high-stake games anymore.

I look forward to the World Series of Poker every
year. As long as they're holding it, you can bet your
damn boots I'll be there. I hope a lot more card players
around the country come out, too. All the local champions usually show up. Some bring $8,000, some bring
$30,000 with them. The more people who want to play,
the merrier, as far as we are concerned. Of course, the
big ones usually eat up the little ones.

I think a lot of people will be in Las Vegas for the
World Series of Poker — rooting for me to win. And
I'll try not to disappoint them; but good Lord, all those
boys are top players. You have to realize you are about
a twelve-to-one underdog against winning the World
Series of Poker when you start with these boys; but I'll
damned sure make it hard for some of them while I'm
there. And they know it, too. Here's hoping I see you
there, neighbor. Maybe you can use these tips of mine,
and knock me out of that fracas. And if you do, all I
can say is you were taught damn well.

Glossary of Gamblese

A.B.C.: ace, deuce, trey.

All in/All out: when a player has all his markers in the pot.

Babies: small cards.

Back seat: the fourth, fifth, sixth or seventh seat to the left of the dealer.

Backed up/Back to back: in a stud game, the first two consecutive cards that are paired. (Two aces, etc.)

Bicycle: ace, deuce, trey, four, five.

Bundle: bankroll of a player.

Burn: to discard the top card from the deck.

Bust hand: an unplayable hand. (See snowball.)

Case ace: last ace in the deck.

Cause a vacancy: to force a player out of the game.

Change-in: money put up by each player in order to participate in a freeze-out type game.

Cheat: any device or gimmick used to improve a player's hand.

Checks/Chips: markers used by players instead of cash money.

Cinch hand: a hand that is impossible to beat.

Cold bluff: having no hand whatsoever, but wanting to appear as though one does.

Commission: fee paid by professional gamblers for use of facilities.

Community cards: those cards placed face up in the center of the table for the use of all players. See hold'em, chapter six.

Concealed hand: one in which cards are not displayed face up where other players may see them.

Cut across: a term used in figuring percentages, when a player does not bother to keep track of cards played that do not directly affect his hand.

Darken the pot: to open before you see your hand; to bet "in the dark," an action common in the game of hold'em.

Dead in the pot: cannot draw a winning card.

Dogs it: throws away the best hand.

Down the river: the seventh card in seven-card stud or razz. This card is played face down.

Double through: to double your chips into another player.

Duck: to throw your hand away.

Eight in the belly: making a middle card straight.

Fall in the center: the exposed cards in hold'em.

Fast game: a game in which the bets are made both frequently and in large amounts.

Fast player: one who bets frequently and in large amounts.

Figuring the price of a pot: Calculating how much the pot will pay you, compared to what you have put into it if you *do* make your hand.

Floor man: shift boss or card room manager.

Flop: the first three exposed cards in hold'em.

Fold: to discard your hand.

Force-in/Forcing the pot: to darken the pot (with raising privileges).

Freeze out: type of game where each player puts in

a certain amount and then cannot quit the game until he has either won everyone else's money or lost all of his own.

Hidden percentage: determined by figuring the odds on making your hand and comparing that with what the pot will pay you if you *do* make your hand.

High rollers: the gamblers who play for big, big stakes.

Hold over: to continually hold the best hand against another player.

Insurance: side bets made away from the table on the outcome of a game that do not affect the pot or the game. The bets can be between onlookers and players or just between players.

In the mouth: first to act.

Kicker: the card that isn't paired in hold'em.

Lay the lash: to make a large bet.

Legging a hand: continually checking the pot.

Limit game: a game in which you may not bet all your chips.

Limping: just calling not raising when you have a good hand.

Locked up: no escape for your opponent.

Mortal cinch: a sure hand.

Move in: to bet all your money.

Nut flush: ace-high flush.

Open-ended straight: where there are eight cards you can draw that will make you a straight.

Out of shape: when a game's stakes become really high.

Overcard: any card that is larger than your highest pair.

Paints: face cards.

Pat: a hand that is complete; when drawing is not necessary.

Peewees: very small cards.

Play back: to raise.

Pocket: hole cards.

Position: your seat at the table in relation to the dealer.

Principle money: money borrowed from one pro by another pro, with a definite time set for repayment.

Rail: the velvet rope separating players from spectators in most casinos.

Rich: when a majority of the cards left in the deck are winners for you.

Rock along: to take it easy, play slow.

Running pair: two consecutive cards of the same denomination.

Sandwich: two players putting another one in the middle in the betting.

Scored pair: in hold'em, the first two down cards or hole cards that are paired.

Scratch up: to beat someone badly.

Senate dealer: a dealer who is not involved in the actual play but who deals all hands in a game.

Shoot the pot up: to make an out-sized bet.

Show down: to show your hand when all your chips are in.

Slicker than a wet gut: to be completely busted.

Snowball: an unplayable hand. (See bust hand.)

Squeak: to complain.

Stash: a player's cash reserve.

Steal a hand: to misrepresent a hand.

Stool a hand: to let everyone know you have a good hand.

Straddle: to double the amount of a force-in.

Strippers: cards with slightly raised edges that can be pulled out of a deck by a cheater or thief.

Table stakes: betting only the amount you have on the table.

Tell: a giveaway trait of players, which can be physical, verbal, or emotional.

Thief: a card cheat.

Tight player: an ultraconservative.
Trapping: checking a good hand.
Trips: three of a kind, a triplet.
Turn: the first three up cards in hold'em. (See flop.)
Under the gun: the first seat to the left of the dealer.
Up front: the first, second or third seat to the left of the dealer.
Wheel: ace, deuce, trey, four, five.

Index

Index

173

Index